Dryden –
On Counselling
Volume 3: Training and Supervision

Dryden –
On Counselling

Volume 3: Training and Supervision

Windy Dryden

Whurr Publishers
London and New Jersey

First published 1991 by

Whurr Publishers Limited
19b Compton Terrace
London N1 2UN
England

British Library Cataloguing in Publication Data

Dryden, Windy
   Dryden on counselling: Vol 3. Training and supervision.
   I. Title
   361.3

   ISBN 1-870332-82-2

Phototypeset by Scribe Design, Gillingham, Kent
Printed in Great Britain by Athenaeum Press Ltd,
Newcastle upon Tyne

Preface

I have been involved in the training and supervision of counsellors for over 15 years. This activity has been conducted in two different forums. First I have been involved with initial counsellor training in a university setting (1) from 1975 to 1984 at the University of Aston where for six of those years I was course tutor on the university's 1-year, full-time postgraduate Diploma in Counselling in Educational Settings course and (2) from 1985 at Goldsmiths' College, University of London where I am course tutor on the Psychology Department's 3-year, part-time, MSc course in Counselling which began in 1989. Second, for the last 12 years I have been involved in training helping professionals in rational–emotive counselling in Britain, USA, Israel and South Africa.

During this period I have written various articles on counsellor training and supervision which are scattered widely in the professional literature. This book seeks to bring together these publications in one volume. For the reader's benefit, I have briefly introduced the chapters in order to provide a context in which each can be understood.

I wish to thank the following for providing permission to reprint material: British Psychological Society (Chapter 3); Hobsons Press (Chapters 4 and 5); Routledge (Chapters 6 and 8) and Sage Publications (Chapters 1 and 2).

Windy Dryden, London
September 1990

Contents

Chapter 1
Key Issues in the Training of Counsellors

This chapter, written with Brian Thorne and published in 1991, outlines some of the key issues that need to be considered when becoming involved in counsellor training. Both Brian and I have been involved in the development and running of the British Association for Counselling's Courses Recognition Group which has been concerned with establishing criteria for the recognition of counsellor training courses. This chapter considers the following issues deemed central by the work of the group:

1. What should be learned and why?
2. Course ethos and philosophical consistency.
3. Selection and resources.

Counselling Comes of Age

When, at the beginning of 1985, the British Association for Counselling set up its Working Group on the Recognition of Counsellor Training Courses it could justifiably be said that counselling had come of age in Britain. Interestingly enough, this event occurred almost 20 years after the first appearance of full-time British counsellor training programmes (in the Universities of Reading and Keele) and some 5 years after the Association's initial scheme for the accreditation of individual counsellors. It seemed that, only after such a lengthy gestation period was the counselling movement sufficiently confident of its own coherence and identity to begin, in earnest, a detailed study of what is required in order to equip someone to fulfil the role of professional counsellor – both an arduous and demanding role. Indeed, it is only comparatively recently that the notion of a counselling profession as such has gained widespread acceptance and, in some circles, the image of the counsellor as a well-meaning but essentially untrained dispenser of comfort and sympathy continues to die hard.

Inevitably, the early training programmes were, to a large extent, in the hands of non-counsellors and consequently the focus of training was often uncertain. Clinical and educational psychologists, social workers and psychiatrists – even psychoanalysts – were involved in the formation of an essentially new kind of therapeutic helper; not unnaturally, they tended to develop models of training that were coloured considerably by their own experience and professional identities. Furthermore, in one sense trainees were made to feel that they were being prepared for an activity which was essentially ancillary, or even inferior, to the more 'professional' work of their trainers. The saving grace in all of this was undoubtedly the frequent presence of American practitioners on the staff of courses developed in British universities during the late 1960s and 1970s. Distinguished professors of counselling, eminent both in practice and scholarship, were keen to take up Fulbright awards in the United Kingdom and, as a result, leading figures in the American counsellor education field made substantial contributions in these early years to the work of counsellor training courses in the Universities of Keele, Reading and Aston-in-Birmingham. Many of the students from these pioneering courses subsequently gained posts of influence, particularly in educational institutions, and it was not long before many of them found themselves taking a training role in addition to their clinical work. The emergence of the British practitioner/trainer had a significant effect on training provision, for it was now increasingly possible to design courses that drew on the actual experience of practising British counsellors, as well as on the well-established tradition from across the Atlantic. Gradually, too, trainers from other disciplines lost their primary role; courses became more clearly focused as they passed into the hands of those who were proud to call themselves counsellors and did not owe their principal allegiance to another profession.

Not all the developments prior to 1985 took place on the campuses of universities and polytechnics. The Marriage Guidance Council (MGC), in particular, was much preoccupied with its training procedures and it is not without significance that the very word 'counsellor' was for many years associated mainly with MGC and its work in the field of marital and relationship difficulties. The increasing demand for the services of marriage guidance counsellors presented the Council with formidable challenges in the training field and it is no small tribute to the dedication and imagination of MG trainers that 'Relate', as it is now called, is currently responding to more clients than ever and that both the numbers and the effectiveness of counsellors operating in this context have increased out of all recognition.

The field of pastoral care and counselling was perhaps the other most influential area for training initiatives. Here, again, many of the pioneers drew extensively on American experience, but the long tradition of social involvement in the British churches meant that there were many Christians, both ordained and lay, who were keen to apply the insights of counselling psychology to the care of hurt and wounded souls in their own communities. Frank Lake and his Clinical Theology Association, and the growth of the Westminster Pastoral Foundation and its affiliated centres, are two of the most striking examples of organisations where commitment to training was and remains central to their operation. Indeed, there are many people in Britain who owe much, if not all, of their counselling training to pastoral agencies of this kind but who would themselves claim little or no Christian allegiance. It is perhaps a mark of the strength of the pastoral care and counselling movement that it has always encouraged cooperation, not only across the Christian denominations, but also with the secular world of counselling and therapy. Significantly, when the British Association for Counselling (BAC) was founded in 1977 it was the Association for Pastoral Care and Counselling (together with the Association for Student Counselling) which agreed to relinquish its previous independence and autonomy in order to ensure the satisfactory 'birth' of the new generic and secular organisation.

The BAC Working Group on the Recognition of Counsellor Training Courses, which met for the first time in January 1985, drew its membership from all the main streams of training experience and expertise described above. There were those who owed their training (and most of their clinical experience) to the universities and polytechnics, whilst others were leading figures from the field of pastoral care and counselling. A third force was provided by a seasoned marriage guidance tutor. In addition, many of the group had experience of training provided both by statutory educational institutions and by private agencies. Indeed, so wide and varied was the experience of the group members that it is perhaps surprising that, 3 years later, they were able to present unanimous recommendations to the British Association concerning the essential ingredients of a counsellor training programme. In the process of their work they had been forced, sometimes painfully, to face all the key issues that the training of counsellors inevitably presents if it is to be undertaken with the seriousness and thoroughness that the counsellor's role undoubtedly requires (British Association for Counselling, 1988).

What Should be Learned and Why?

Self-exploration

For the counsellor trainer, one of the most daunting issues which has to be faced at the outset of any course is the fact that if things go well they will not go smoothly. The reason for this is that training, if it is to be effective, must involve a high degree of self-exploration on the part of trainees with the aim of increasing their self-awareness and self-knowledge. Even in those therapeutic traditions where the emphasis is on clients' behavioural change or the modification of cognitive processes, it is nevertheless accepted that an unaware counsellor leading an unexamined life is likely to be a liability rather than an asset. By definition, however, self-exploration leads to new discoveries and often sudden movement into unknown psychological terrain. Some of these developments are likely to be disturbing and disorienting with the result that almost all trainees, at some stage of their training, are likely to experience periods of distress or bewilderment and may even at times become subject to incapacitating anxiety or depression. Notoriously, too, relationships with spouses and other family members are liable to undergo considerable upheaval or even to founder altogether. The trainer is therefore presented with two closely related tasks: how to ensure that trainees are given adequate opportunity for self-exploration and how to establish the kind of structure that will hold and support those who find themselves struggling with new and unexpected discoveries about themselves?

There are those who believe that these requirements can only be met by ensuring that every trainee undergoes personal therapy as an obligatory part of training. Without such provision, it is argued, there can be no guarantee that the trainee will confront, in a systematic and thorough manner, those areas of his or her life and personality that are a potential source of difficulty or conflict. What is more, an insistence on personal therapy has the additional advantage of making sure that the trainee has a real and substantial experience of being in the client's chair. These are powerful arguments but not all trainers are convinced by them. Those who oppose obligatory personal therapy (and there are none, we believe, who would question the value of personal therapy which is sought voluntarily by a trainee) do so on the grounds that the therapy relationship itself can serve as a means of evading important interpersonal difficulties which may be part of the trainee's experience both within the course and in his or her personal life. Central to this criticism is the fear that some trainees will see personal therapy as *the* arena for self-exploration (within limits) and will feel entitled to remain somewhat aloof and withdrawn in other areas of the training programme. Those who espouse this point of view will place heavy emphasis on the concept of the training group itself – or a subgroup within it – as the chief therapeutic environment for the development of self-awareness. In this model, the trainees are encouraged to see the course community as the context, both for self-exploration and for finding support in times of particular difficulty. Trainers, supervisors and personal therapists, where they exist, may have important roles to play in offering additional or specific help, but they are not there so that trainees can 'siphon off' important personal material that belongs more appropriately to the group as a whole. It should be remembered that membership of a group can itself be a powerful trigger for self-exploration. Groups and organisations frequently present individuals with new challenges and new threats which can only be faced by a willingness to be open to the strengths and vulnerabilities that are thereby revealed. In this way, the course community may well serve a dual function: it can be the therapeutic arena for facing those very insights into the self which it has itself provoked.

Clearly self-exploration can occur in a variety of different contexts and indeed, for some trainees, the opportunity to be at quiet with themselves as they study for an essay or reflect on a day's work is more productive than the most dramatic group encounter. For the trainer, however, there can be no assumption that such self-exploration will take place automatically. The course design and the apportioning of time must reflect the high priority given to ensuring that such exploration is central to the counsellor's apprenticeship and not an optional extra. What is more, a course, through its structure, needs to recognise that many and possibly all trainees will experience pain and distress as they gradually confront themselves more honestly and courageously: they should not be left with nowhere to go and nobody to whom they can turn when such testing times occur.

Work with clients

However difficult it may be to believe, there are counselling courses where trainees never meet a client. The reasoning behind such a bizarre state of affairs is that fellow trainees are deemed to constitute the clientèle and to provide more than enough material for counselling practice. The inadequacy of such reasoning is not difficult to expose for it is clear that trainees on a course are unlikely to be motivated by the various and often pressing needs that bring 'normal' clients to the counsellor's door. Even in those instances where genuinely felt concerns and difficulties are experienced, the fact that the 'client' is likely to be well known to the 'counsellor' introduces a factor into the therapeutic relationship which strikingly distinguishes it from the usual case-load of the practising counsellor in the ordinary course of events. Indeed, it is not uncommon for many counsellors to refuse in principle to counsel those who are friends of even passing acquaintances.

The willingness of some course organisers to settle for this unsatisfactory method of providing clients for trainees is undoubtedly prompted by the difficulty that often arises in attempting to set up a valid counselling experience for course members. It is not always easy to persuade counselling agencies to welcome trainees and, where students themselves are left with the responsibility of arranging their own placements, they may find that they carry little credibility. The issues here are complex. Clearly, it is essential that trainees have clients but it is also understandable that counselling agencies or general practitioners, for example, should be hesitant about letting unskilled beginners loose on their clients or patients.

Questions that have to be addressed include the point at which trainees should first be permitted to see clients. From the trainer's point of view, the sooner the student has some 'real' experience, the more likely it is that he or she will be able to relate theory to practice. However, it could be argued that, from the client's point of view and that of a counselling agency, it is of considerable importance that the trainee is already in possession of a modicum of theoretical knowledge and has had some opportunity to develop basic counselling skills. Whichever policy is adopted, it is clearly crucial that close and frequent supervision is provided for the trainee and that his or her case-load is kept to two or three clients at any one time for at least the initial stages of the training programme. A policy which dictates that a trainee should have only one client at a time is more questionable for there is a danger that the single client can become of such critical significance to the trainee that there is an over-investment in securing a successful 'outcome'.

The provision of supervision is often fraught with problems. Inexperienced trainees are naturally anxious and lacking in self-confidence and may require frequent reassurance. The accessibility of the supervisor, both in person and on the telephone, is of major importance and, if an agency is also providing field supervision, it is not in the least helpful to a trainee if the styles and even the therapeutic orientations of the two supervisors concerned are widely divergent. If a course only provides group supervision, it is important that the group is small enough and the sessions of sufficient duration for all members to present their work regularly and in depth.

It is often claimed by students on teacher training courses that the real learning occurs on teaching practice. Much the same could be said of the counselling practice, and for this reason it is desirable that trainees have the opportunity to work with a variety of clients during this training period and to experience both short- and long-term counselling relationships. The supervision requirements for such practice are considerable and there are obvious resource implications which will be considered later.

The acquisition of counselling skills

Fellow trainees may not constitute an appropriate source for clientèle but they undoubtedly provide the best possible milieu for developing counselling skills. Skills training offers trainees the opportunity to isolate and analyse specific responses to clients in a way which is scarcely possible within the context of a normal counselling relationship. Such training is often enhanced by the use of audio and video equipment which permits the trainee to carry out a detached exploration of small segments of interaction and to investigate the impact of particular verbal responses and the power of non-verbal communication. The skills which are being developed may vary from one therapeutic orientation to another, but the capacity to form a therapeutic alliance with clients will be common to them all. The person-centred trainee, for example, is likely to devote much attention to increasing the repertoire of empathic responses whereas the cognitive–behavioural counsellor may be keen to practise interventions which impinge on self-defeating thinking and behavioural patterns. Both trainees, however, through the intensive practice of specific skills, will be familiarising themselves with the essential tools of their trade, but will be doing this in a context where the skills cannot be divorced from attitudes and from a consideration of the relationship which is being forged with the client. At least, this must be the hope, because the danger of skills training which is conducted in a vacuum is that the trainee can emerge at the end armed with a kit of techniques and strategies but little capacity to develop the kind of relationship where those skills can be creatively employed. Trainers of all traditions have constantly to be on their guard so that they do not encourage the emergence of clever technicians rather than sensitive counsellors.

Counselling skills training is likely to take up much of the time in the formal timetabling of a course and it presents several operational difficulties. For most trainees, it is likely to be one of the most threatening of their activities and has therefore to be approached with delicacy and with a regard for individual differences. Some students, for example, take readily to role-playing or to appearing on a video, whereas others must work through much anxiety before they are ready to risk themselves in these ways. Trainers have to exhibit both firmness and gentleness if all participants are eventually to benefit from the various learning situations. Much sensitivity is also demanded of trainers if they are to assist trainees to give each other honest feed-back during skills sessions. In the initial stages of training, it is both natural and desirable that emphasis should be laid on the positive aspects of a trainee's counselling behaviour, but later on it becomes a hindrance to growth if more critical comment is always withheld out of fear of hurting the trainee or undermining his or her confidence. It is often the trainer who must first model the kind of feed-back that can incorporate both positive and negative reactions without losing a deep respect and caring for the trainee whose work is being observed. Once a training group has established a climate where such feed-back is both offered and welcomed, there is no limit to the learning that can develop in counselling skills sessions.

Counselling theory and academic content

Counselling courses which first developed in university settings usually found themselves saddled with academic requirements and regulations that were scarcely conducive to effective training. Frequent written work was often required during the course together with lengthy formal examinations at the end. Courses which have developed outside traditional academic institutions have tended to err in the opposite direction and have placed almost exclusive importance on experiential and practical work. It is clear, however, that counsellors who have a poor theoretical understanding of their work are likely to lose their heads (and their hearts) when confronted by difficult clients or particularly complex dilemmas. Experiential learning which is unsupported by sound theoretical understanding is likely, after a while, to leave the trainee confused or incapable of describing and analysing the processes he or she is experiencing with clients. At the very least, there needs to be a sufficient emphasis on reading and written work to ensure that students are able to clarify philosophical and theoretical concepts and to apply them to their practical counselling work.

As with counselling skills, trainers need to be aware that, for some trainees, 'academic' work arouses acute anxiety and deep feelings of inadequacy, but here again course members are likely to be able to offer each other considerable support once initial fears of insensitive criticism have been allayed. For some students it may well be that progress in their ability to conceptualise their work and to discuss it intelligently with professionals from allied fields will constitute a major arena for building self-respect and enhancing self-confidence. The need to be able to communicate across professional boundaries also dictates that time is given to studying the work of such professions as psychiatry, clinical psychology and social work. It is likely, too, that many courses will be offering a training in one specific school of counselling but this 'majoring' in a particular tradition should not preclude a comparative study of other forms of counselling. The psychodynamic counsellor who is ignorant, for example, of the person-centred approach or of cognitive therapy is scarcely in a favourable position to enter into constructive dialogue with colleagues from those other traditions or to be able to offer effective guidance to clients who may wish to be referred elsewhere. The question of whether initial training courses *should* offer only one approach to counselling is perhaps itself debatable, although it is doubtful whether, in most cases, the time factor would allow in-depth training in the practice of more than one orientation. This, however, is a separate question from the comparative study of counselling theories and methodologies. In a field where it is increasingly evident that an ecumenical spirit is abroad, it would seem to be of the utmost importance that trainees do not emerge from their courses with blinkered minds and no knowledge of therapeutic traditions other than the one in which they have been immersed. What is more, there needs to be a thorough study of those ethical and other professional issues that concern all counsellors whatever their theoretical 'stable'.

Counselling does not take place in a vacuum and a training course needs to acknowledge this by drawing on relevant social science disciplines in order to illuminate the systems in which people live. Social, cultural, ethnic and political issues are but some of the ingredients of the kind of exploration that is required if justice is to be done to the study of the environment; this in its different ways may profoundly affect the lives of clients. Also it cannot be taken for granted that every trainee has a clear understanding of human development and the nature of the human personality. Some counselling theories explicitly incorporate such conceptualisations, but there is a strong case for presenting contrasting models so that trainees can wrestle with the combined and perhaps conflicting insights offered by biology, psychology, sociology and theology. In short, a counselling course which travels so light on academic content that it fails to do justice to at least some of the issues raised above is scarcely equipping its trainees for the kind of discourse that may well be demanded of them both by potential clients and by colleagues in allied disciplines.

The Course Ethos and Philosophical Consistency

Part of the discomfort that those in some counselling courses based in educational institutions have experienced arises from the ethos of competition, assessment and evaluation which not uncommonly prevails in such places and which, if anything, has grown more pronounced in recent years. Such an ethos is not conducive to the creation of a climate for learning where trainees can begin to take risks that inevitably render them vulnerable to the scrutiny and judgement of others. Central to most counselling approaches is a deep respect for the client and a willingness to understand and accept him or her without adverse judgement. If trainees themselves experience attitudes and behaviours from their trainers which are grossly at variance with such a philosophy of respect and acceptance, it is likely that they will become angry and disillusioned at such a blatant discrepancy and will justifiably suspect trainers of irresponsible inconsistency or, at worst, of manifest hypocrisy.

There are important issues here which have a bearing on almost every aspect of a training programme. Trainers are at all times models of the counselling approach that they represent and the way they lecture or facilitate small groups or conduct private interviews will be construed by trainees in the light of the practice and philosophy that they profess to advocate. This places a burden of expectation on the trainer which is not always easy to carry, but there is no way in which this can be avoided. There can be few areas of vocational education where the credibility of the trainer is so much at stake in almost every word that is uttered and every action performed, however small and apparently inconsequential.

The issue of consistency may have profound implications for the way in which a course is structured. If, for example, the counselling approach which is being taught lays great emphasis on the trustworthiness of the client and on his or her ability to discover inner resources, it makes little sense if the course structure is totally determined by the trainers in advance. It follows from the underlying theory that the trainees will increasingly be capable of discovering their own way forward and of generating their own resources. If opportunity is not provided for this kind of development, then a glaring inconsistency rapidly becomes apparent. An even more sensitive area is likely to be the process of assessment and the methods employed for determining a student's eventual competence to practise. Courses where all the assessment power is retained in the hands of the trainers are unlikely to be in perfect harmony with the philosophy of the therapeutic approach which is being taught (unless perhaps it is a course in directive hypnosis!), and yet in some conventional institutions it may be inevitable, due to statutes and regulations, that boards of examiners retain the absolute power to pass or fail. The tensions in situations such as this can be extremely unhealthy and it may be incumbent on counsellor trainers to mount a concerted campaign on inappropriate institutional procedures with all the backing that can be obtained from the British Association for Counselling and other profession-al bodies. However, not all the blame can be placed on academic conservatism, as clearly evidenced by the fact that training courses run by private agencies and institutions are not always blameless when it comes to assessment procedures. The issues of power and status are complex and it is a formidable task to develop modes of evaluation that are at one and the same time sensitive to the trustworthiness of trainees, the insight and experience of trainers and the interests of future clients. The task is not impossible but it demands a level of honesty and humility that is seldom achieved in any profession. The appointment of an external consultant is almost certainly an essential ingredient in any process which is to stand much chance of evolving an assessment procedure that will be fully consistent with the underlying philosophy of the training being offered.

Selection and Resources

Selection

It may seem strange to leave the question of who should be accepted for counselling training to the final section of this discussion. However, perhaps the issue can be more realistically explored in the light of the course content and the demands of the training described above. It would seem that the prospective trainee needs to be resourceful and resilient enough to embark upon a process that will require intense and continuing self-exploration, an ability to work with a range of clients, a willingness to participate fully in counselling skills work that involves exposure to the scrutiny of others, a commitment to substantial academic study (often perfectly possible for those without high academic qualifications) and a preparedness to face almost inevitable disturbance and change in his or her personal life. This is a still challenge indeed and not one to be undertaken lightly.

The task faced by selectors is rendered more difficult by the fact that almost all applicants are motivated and enthusiastic. What is more they often present as highly sensitive people with a genuine desire to help others. References can sometimes indicate areas that require further investigation, but more often than not they reinforce this impression of a sensitive, thoughtful person with high motivation and well-developed altruistic feelings. In the past some courses have employed personality tests or have set up somewhat daunting group situations where applicants can display their interpersonal skills in discussion with each other. There is little evidence to suggest that such methods are particularly successful. The issues which need to be explored are more difficult to get at for they are essentially concerned with the applicant's state of readiness for the training experience. Such readiness is dependent upon the state of the person's internal and external world and both are notoriously difficult to explore in depth during a selection process. It would seem, however, that many would-be trainees are seeking a personal growth experience rather than a training course and this is an issue that needs to be brought to the surface if at all possible. This is not usually a straightforward matter because applicants who are not prepared to develop as people during training are also unlikely candidates. The issue here is one of balance and priorities. The appropriateness of enrolling students who are in personal therapy or have only recently finished a period of therapy is related to the personal growth issue. Clearly, the experience of being a client is invaluable for a trainee and, as we have seen, there are many who believe that such an experience should be an integral part of training anyway. However, it is not unusual for those in therapy to be in a particularly vulnerable state or to be emerging from a period of considerable fragility or perturbation. The start on a training course may actually re-open wounds which are only just beginning to heal. As far as the external world is concerned, it is not uncommon for applicants to be in difficult relationships (often marital) from which a training course promises an escape and the prospect of new persons with whom to relate more congenially. Some applicants, too, may be in difficult work situations where there is no job satisfaction and little prospect of improvement. Such factors are not automatically contraindicators of suitability for training, but they certainly raise a number of questions to which selectors need to be attentive. Candidates who seem to have little support from their families and friends are also likely to be at risk, as are those who have not thought through the implications of the energy, time and money involved in undertaking a training of such length and intensity. There is probably no fully satisfactory way of selecting trainees, but it is certainly a process that requires the greatest of care and in which the candidate's world needs to be tapped into beyond a superficial level. Certainly it should never be undertaken by one selector alone.

Resources

There can be few training roles as taxing as that of the counsellor trainer for he or she is likely to become deeply involved in the lives of many candidates who will be wrestling with major challenges in their personal and professional development. There are likely to be many crises of confidence among trainees and periods of confusion and debilitating self-doubt. Not only does the trainer have to be a sensitive companion to persons experiencing turmoil of this kind, but he or she has also to perform the multiple tasks of the lecturer, group facilitator, skills trainer and scholarly academic. In addition, this type of work has to be maintained at an intensive level over a lengthy period of time – no counselling course worthy of the name would be of shorter duration than 1 year full-time or 2–3 years part-time. One immediate implication of the demanding nature of the role is that counselling courses must have a high ratio of staff to students. No course should be run by one solitary individual and the core staff should probably be in the ratio of at least one to every eight to ten trainees. Also there will clearly be a need for a range of supervision opportunities which may well involve many more staff. It is unlikely, too, that a small core staff will, between them, be able adequately to cover all aspects of the desirable curriculum, and it is likely that several guest lecturers and tutors will have to be engaged at different stages. Core staff members should themselves be practising counsellors – there can be few occupations where the continuing interaction between practice and theory is of such fundamental importance in the training process. The trainer who is no longer practising as a counsellor will quickly lose the immediacy of experience that provides the major stimulus for creativity and is the principal source of his or her credibility in the eyes of trainees.

Counselling courses make heavy demands on staff time and energy, and the sheer number of staff required, if effective supervision is to be provided, inevitably means that staff salaries will make considerable inroads into institutional budgets or on students' own financial resources where courses do not receive institutional subsidy. There seems to be no way round this unfortunate situation which suggests that counselling training of high quality may well have already become inaccessible to those without substantial financial resources. It is to be hoped that some institutions at least will find it possible to make generous subsidies for counselling training, and that charitable foundations will be increasingly prepared to support trainees without the necessary financial resources. If this does not prove to be so, the counselling world will undoubtedly be deprived of many gifted practitioners especially from the ethnic minority groups in this country.

Apart from staff, the resource requirements of counselling courses are modest. There is a need for comfortable and flexible accommodation where it is comparatively easy to switch from one-to-one to small group to large group activities. For most therapeutic orientations, training will be greatly enhanced by the ready availability of video and audio equipment and there is no escape from the fact that a reputable library is a sine qua non. In a field where changes are often rapid and where innovation can occur in unexpected quarters, it is highly desirable that there is ready access to at least some of the leading professional journals. When all is said and done, however, the chief resource for every trainee remains the trainer. It is this person who by his or her integrity and skill will enable the trainee to move from timorous beginnings to the humble confidence of the fledgling counsellor. Perhaps, in the last analysis, the key issue which surpasses all the others in importance is the nature of the man or woman who is bold enough to undertake a task where success ultimately depends, not simply on knowledge or even on experience, but on a quality of being that can continue to offer support at those moments when the trainee is on the point of abandoning the struggle to enter so impossible a profession.

Reference

BRITISH ASSOCIATION FOR COUNSELLING (1988). *Recognition of Counselling Training Courses*, Rugby.

Chapter 2
Approaches to the Training of Counsellors

This chapter, written with Brian Thorne and published in expanded form in 1991, takes as its theme how counsellor trainers approach their task. Focusing on the four topics outlined in the previous chapter and listed under the heading 'What should be learned and why?', the chapter considers the advantages and disadvantages of training approaches designed to:

1. Foster trainee self-exploration.
2. Facilitate the supervision of trainees' work with their clients.
3. Promote the development of trainees' counselling skills.
4. Teach counselling theory and related academic material.

Introduction

In the previous chapter, it was argued that initial counselling training courses should provide trainees with learning opportunities in four main areas: (1) self-exploration; (2) supervised work with clients; (3) the acquisition of counselling skills; and (4) counselling theory and relevant academic material. In this chapter, the focus will be on *how* this might be done, i.e. *approaches* to initial counsellor training will be considered.

However, before embarking on a detailed discussion of these issues, the following points need to be borne in mind throughout the chapter.

1. The four areas outlined above are not discrete. Rather they should be seen as interrelated components of a course's curriculum. Whilst work with clients should be the central concern of any course designed to train counselling *practitioners*, the success of this is predicated on the following: (i) that trainees bring *themselves* to the work and as such they should be aware of and have an opportunity to overcome ways in which their personal agendas may interfere with effective counselling; (ii) that counselling is a skilful enterprise and that effective counselling skills need to be acquired and internalised; and (iii) that

effective counsellors are guided by appropriate theoretical frameworks and salient knowlege (e.g. of client problems).

Indeed, even the seemingly unrelated areas of theoretical knowledge and self-exploration are in fact crucially linked and thus trainees should be given opportunities to explore the personal implications of academic material. For example, if the research literature on anger is the focus of academic study, trainees should be encouraged to reflect on their own experience of being angry and explore both how this experience can be informed by research and how the research could possibly be illuminated or refuted by their experience.

2. The choice of methods of training depends crucially upon the goals of that training. Furthermore, the goals of counsellor training will be inextricably linked with the trainers' view of the effective practitioner. Thus, on a person-centred counselling training course, the effective practitioner is one who is able to offer clients consistently high levels of the three core facilitative conditions, namely empathy, acceptance and genuineness. The goal of such a course then would be to 'graduate' trainees who are able to do this and the training method question then becomes 'How can we best help students to respond genuinely to clients with empathy and acceptance?'.

3. The choice of methods of training counsellors will also depend upon who determines the curriculum. There are some counselling courses that are founded on the concept of self-directed learning. The philosophy which underpins such courses postulates that, since effective counselling provides an environment where clients can direct their own learning, effective training should provide the same type of environment for trainees. Thus, trainees on such courses are encouraged to set their own learning objectives and choose how these objectives can best be met. It is likely that experiential methods will be used more frequently on such courses than on those where the curriculum is determined more by trainers than by trainees, this being a situation that often prevails when the latter are validated by academic institutions.

4. There is increasing evidence that effective counselling occurs when there is a strong working alliance between client and counsellor (see Dryden, 1989). This alliance has three major components: bonds, goals and tasks. Extrapolating from this evidence our hypothesis is that successful training depends on a strong working alliance between trainers and trainees (and indeed among trainees themselves). When trainers use alliance theory to inform their approach to training, a number of questions become salient: Can trainees see how participating in a particular training method (task) will lead to the achievement of their own training objectives (goal)? To what extent are trainees' training goals congruent with the training goals of the course? What

is the quality of the relationship (bond) between trainers and trainees and among trainees themselves, and how does this affect trainees' engagement with and learning from their tasks as trainees?

Whilst the emphasis in this chapter is on the task domain of counsellor training, the other two domains of the alliance should always be borne in mind when counsellor training *as a whole* is being considered. In particular, the success of counsellor training is probably intimately related to the quality of the relationship between trainees and trainers. It is also clear that the assessment processes employed during a course may have major implications for this relationship as indeed they have for much else within the training experience.

Following on from the above points, the focus will now be on how counsellor training may be approached in the four areas outlined at the beginning of the chapter and, in particular the advantages and disadvantages of the methods discussed will be considered.

Self-exploration

As pointed out in the previous chapter 'an unaware counsellor leading an unexamined life is likely to be a liability rather than an asset' as a practitioner. Indeed there is some research evidence to suggest that client outcome is positively associated with lack of emotional disturbance in the counsellor (Beutler, Crago and Arizmendi, 1986). How, then, do counsellor training courses *formally* encourage trainee self-exploration?; the word formally is stressed here because it is recognised that trainee personal growth can and does take place through informal contact with trainers and fellow trainees.

Personal therapy

A traditional approach to trainee self-exploration has been to have trainees engage in their own personal therapy either as a requirement for course participation or as a valued but voluntary additional activity. This approach is particularly embraced by psychodynamically oriented counsellor trainers whose view is that trainee counsellors need to be acutely aware of their own personal dynamics, so that they can distinguish between healthy and unhealthy countertransference reactions to their clients (Jacobs, 1988).

Courses vary in the degree of freedom they give trainees with regard to their choice of personal therapist; this varies from offering total freedom to providing trainees with a list of 'acceptable' therapists. This raises the issue of whether the orientation of trainees' personal therapists should be

congruent with the orientation of the course. On balance, such congruence is probably advantageous, otherwise trainees may become overly
confused by the possible discrepancy between what they are being taught
about counselling on their course and what they are learning about
counselling from their personal therapy.

However, given that research has shown that 33 per cent of trainees
have unsatisfactory personal therapy experiences (Aveline, 1990), trainees
should be encouraged to delay commitment to personal therapy until they
have found a counsellor with whom they feel they can work productively.
This means that trainers should encourage trainees to 'shop around' until
they have found a counsellor who has a high degree of empathy with the
likely experiences of trainee counsellors during the duration of their
course. This, however, should *not* be a member of the training staff. In our
opinion, when trainers serve as personal therapists to their trainees the
fact that the latter will be evaluated in other areas of the course by the
former does not ordinarily assist the creation of the best climate for
fostering self-exploration. (Also, it is in violation of the BAC Code of Ethics
and Practice for Trainers.)

An important issue arises when the focus of trainees' personal therapy
is considered. Should trainees allow themselves full rein to discuss
whatever they choose in their personal therapy or should the focus be on
the experiences and implications of being a trainee? Whilst the former is
the norm, it is worth experimenting with the latter. This might be one way
to boost the correlation between personal therapy and therapist effectiveness, for at present there is equivocal evidence that having personal
therapy improves one's effectiveness as a counsellor or therapist (Aveline,
1990).

Personal development groups

A common feature of many counsellor training courses is the personal
development group (PDG) which is offered either in addition to personal
therapy or instead of it. The major advantage of PDGs over personal
therapy is that they offer trainees an opportunity to explore their
relationships with one another and to benefit from the curative factors that
groups provide (e.g. universality, cohesion and interpersonal feedback). In
particular, they provide a forum for the airing and resolution of
interpersonal conflict among trainees which may otherwise spill over to
other parts of the course and thereby inhibit learning.

The major disadvantage of PDGs is that they may not be the best forum
for self-exploration for all trainees. Some trainees, like some clients, require
the individual attention that the area of individual counselling provides
(Dryden, 1990).

The effective leader of PDGs should (1) be an experienced group facilitator, (2) be sensitive to the needs and stage of personal development of trainee counsellors, (3) have a therapeutic orientation congruent with that of the course and (4) not be involved in the formal evaluation of trainees.

It has been argued that trainees' personal therapists and PDG leaders should ideally be unconcerned with the formal evaluation of trainees. It goes without saying that these therapists/leaders should maintain confidentiality with respect to their trainee clients. Whether or not this confidentiality should be absolute is debatable. There is a case for a course leader being alerted to the fact that a trainee is severely distressed and perhaps potentially harmful to clients. Frequently, trainees will realise this themselves and, with or without prompting from their therapist, discuss the situation with their tutor. On the rare occurrence where a trainee refuses to acknowledge this state of affairs, the therapist, or PDG leader, may choose to break confidentiality and inform the course tutor in order to safeguard the welfare of the trainees' clients. If this is going to be the case, trainees need to be informed in advance of the limits of confidentiality.

Journal work

It is now common practice for trainees to be asked to keep personal journals of their experiences on their training courses. What varies among courses is the amount of structure the participants are given within which to explore these experiences. Some tutors formally train students in intense journal methods (e.g. Progoff, 1975), whilst others explain broadly the purpose of keeping such journals (i.e. to explore and reflect upon personal and professional development) and give minimal specific guidance on how this might be done or what might be covered.

If trainers respect individual differences concerning the form of a journal (e.g. some trainees prefer to keep a verbal record on audio-tape) and if trainees engage in this task regularly, it can be a powerful stimulus for private reflection and self-exploration. In particular it is a helpful format for setting and reviewing training objectives. However, some trainees require the presence of another person to engage meaningfully in self-exploration and for these the tape recording of co-counselling sessions (when the trainee is the client) can be a valuable alternative. Other trainees may be constrained by the knowledge that their tutors have access to their journals and thus, on some courses, it is a requirement that journals be kept but they do not have to be handed in for appraisal.

Whilst personal therapy, PDGs and journal work are the main approaches to fostering trainee self-exploration on counselling training courses, several other methods are commonly employed which will be briefly noted.

Other approaches

Peer counselling

In this situation, trainees counsel one another for an agreed time period in a co-counselling format (Evison and Horobin, 1988). This can be done within or outside the context of counsellor skills training. Whilst this should never be the only form of self-exploration on a course, it can be very helpful where the trainees concerned trust each other. It is less helpful when that trust is lacking and where one or both trainees have poorly developed counselling skills.

Personal tutorials

Unless a training course is particularly well endowed with staff, it is unlikely that trainees will receive many individual personal tutorials. When they do occur they can provide a very useful format for tutors and trainees to explore the latter's personal and professional development. If the trainee respects the tutor and the tutor offers both positive feed-back and suggestions for future development, this can be the stimulus for healthy self-exploration and growth. However, when the tutor just gives negative feed-back this can be very discouraging for the trainee.

Whilst courses ideally should provide regular opportunities for trainees to give feed-back on their experiences of the course (usually in a group setting), the personal tutorial can also be used for eliciting individual trainee feed-back. When this is non-defensively received and taken seriously, it can foster, in the trainee, the empowering feeling that he or she can have an influence on the course's future development.

Community and residential meetings

On many training programmes, opportunities are provided for the course to meet regularly as a community and occasionally in a residential setting for an extended time period. Whether or not the stated purpose of such meetings is for personal growth, there is no doubt that, although often anxiety provoking, such experiences can have a powerful positive effect on trainees. However, if led unskilfully, such meetings also have the potential to be damaging, particularly if scape-goating is allowed to occur unchecked.

In closing, and as noted at the beginning of this chapter, the major areas of training are interdependent. As such, much useful self-exploration can be initiated in the skills, supervision and academic components of training courses if trainees are given the time and opportunity to reflect on the personal implications of what is learned in these other contexts.

upervised Work with Clients

It was argued at the beginning of this chapter that work with clients forms the central core of courses designed to train counselling practitioners. It follows that regular supervision of this work is crucial. However, the success of this supervision depends upon a number of factors. First, trainees need to be deemed ready to see clients. Thus, before seeing clients, trainees need to demonstrate an emerging capacity to (1) respond consistently to clients from the latter's frame of reference; (2) communicate empathic understanding of clients' concerns; (3) be genuine and non-defensive in their interactions with clients; (4) demonstrate unconditional acceptance of their clients; (5) maintain appropriate confidentiality; and (6) demonstrate a working knowledge of severe psychopathology so that they can refer on clients who can be better served by other therapeutic intervention. It is likely that much initial work in counselling skills groups and personal development groups will be devoted to preparing trainees to demonstrate 'readiness' on these criteria.

Secondly, successful supervision depends upon a good working alliance being established between the trainee, the agency where the trainee will see clients and the training course. For example, if the course requires that the trainee tape record his or her counselling sessions (with, of course, the agreement of the client), the trainee needs to accept this (before entering the course). Also the agency needs to give permission for this to happen before the start of the placement. Thus, a productive channel of communication between the trainee, the course tutor and the agency needs to be established and maintained throughout the time that the trainee is on placement. If problems do arise during the placement, there also has to be a forum in which such problems can be discussed and resolved.

Thirdly, appropriate selection of clients to be counselled by trainees needs to be undertaken which takes into account the stage of development reached by each trainee as a counsellor.

Fourthly, the counselling orientation of supervisors needs to be congruent with the orientation of the course. Supervision can be doomed from the outset if, for example, a psychodynamic supervisor is assigned to a trainee who is being trained in cognitive–behavioural counselling.

After outlining the above pre-conditions for effective supervision, the way in which such supervision may be approached will be considered with particular emphasis on methods which focus on what *actually* goes on in counselling sessions and those which focus on *discussion* of what goes on in counselling sessions.

The 'actual data' approach to supervision

When the focus of supervision is on what actually goes on between trainee counsellor and client, the supervisor needs access to an accurate record of this interaction. Whilst psychodynamic supervisors often encourage and train their supervisees to take detailed verbatim 'process notes' immediately after counselling sessions, this method has not been shown to provide a reliable record of the interaction (Covner, 1944; Muslin, Thurnblad and Meschel, 1981). Thus use of audio recordings, video recordings with an audio channel, or live interviews are necessary if actual data are to be obtained.

When audio and video recordings form the basis of supervision, the focus is frequently on how trainees actually respond to client material. Feed-back can be given to trainees concerning verbal and non-verbal interventions that are both helpful and unhelpful. With respect to the latter, trainees can be encouraged to consider alternative interventions which could have been more enabling.

In addition, the review of audio and video recordings in supervision can provide a structure for discussion of the trainee's experiences at various stages of the interview. Methods such as interpersonal process recall (see Kagan, 1984; Kagan and Kagan, 1990) and brief structured recall (see Elliott and Shapiro, 1988) can be of additional use here. When such recordings are used in this way, the focus of supervision often changes to a discussion of what went on in the session.

Audio and video recordings can also be used to discuss what the trainee intended by a particular response (Hill and O'Grady, 1985). What the supervisor does here is to stop the tape after every verbal response made by the trainee, who is asked to recall what he or she intended by the response. (See Dryden, 1984, p. 358, for a list of therapist intentions. This list can be given to trainees to stimulate recall.)

The advantage of the use of audio and video recordings in supervision is that they allow the supervisor access to what actually went on in a session and thus permit him or her to give trainees feed-back concerning actual interventions made. They are then best used when the focus of supervision is on specific counselling responses and on the skill element of counselling. Such recordings are often used by supervisors who embrace person-centred (and other humanistic) approaches, transactional analysis and cognitive–behavioural counselling, but are not used frequently by psychodynamic supervisors whose concern is much more about understanding the dynamics of what goes on in counselling.

The disadvantage of such methods is that supervisors can easily get bogged down in micro issues to the neglect of macro issues, such as understanding the client and the dynamics of the counsellor–client relationship, treatment planning and case management. Additionally, the use of such methods often leads to trainees becoming self-conscious, a phenomenon that usually disappears with their continued use. However, for such trainees and those with acute performance anxiety their use is contraindicated until this anxiety can be reduced (see Dryden, 1987 and Chapter 6).

Live supervision is a method that requires the supervisor to watch and listen to the trainee conducting an actual counselling session (with the client's informed consent) while being able to talk to the trainee via a 'bug in the ear', giving immediate feed-back on the counselling and making suggestions for possible intervention. The main advantages of this method lie in the fact that immediate feed-back can be given and that trainees can immediately implement their supervisors' suggestions and monitor the effects of their interventions. Its main disadvantage lies in the fact that it can be unduly distracting for both the counsellor and client.

The case discussion approach to supervision (see also Chapter 4)

In case discussion, the supervisory focus is precisely on those issues that 'actual data' methods tend to neglect. The emphasis here is more on macro than on micro counselling issues. Discussion tends to centre on under-standing the client and understanding the relationship between counsellor and client from a broader perspective than can be achieved with 'actual data' supervision methods. In addition, treatment planning and case management issues are frequently the focus of concern in case discussion. As mentioned above, psychodynamic supervisors make much use of this supervision approach, focusing particularly on possible unconscious factors that influence the counselling and on issues of transference and countertransference.

Case discussion supervisors differ concerning how much structure they encourage trainees to bring to the discussion (for an example of a structured approach to case discussion see Jacobs, 1981). They all, however, tend to stress the possible presence of parallel process (where the dynamics of the supervisor–trainee interaction may parallel the dynamics of the trainee counsellor–client interaction – see McNeill and Worthen, 1989).

The major disadvantage of case discussion as an approach to supervision is that it cannot focus on what *actually* transpired in the counselling session. Thus, it is not an appropriate method if the focus of concern is on counselling skills.

The reader will probably have anticipated the following conclusion, namely that the use of *both* case discussion *and* 'actual data' approaches to supervision should be employed. The important task of the supervisor here is to use the approach that is best suited to the focus of concern being addressed at any point in the supervisory relationship. To encourage trainees to see the value of *both* these approaches, it is very helpful for supervisors to discuss occasionally one or two of their own cases and to play tapes from these cases (if indeed they make them).

Training in Counselling Skills (see also Chapter 3)

Attempts to demystify the process of counselling so that researchers could study the relationship between counsellor behaviour and client outcome began in earnest with the publication of Truax and Carkhuff's (1967) seminal work. These authors developed scales which detailed, more than anyone had done previously, specific features of the core conditions of counsellor empathy, unconditional positive regard and congruence.

This landmark work spawned a number of similar (but not identical) approaches to conceptualise counselling as a process of different points during which counsellors require different skills. Furthermore, the originators of these approaches (e.g. Carkhuff, 1987; Ivey, 1988; Egan, 1990) developed training 'packages' designed to train counsellors in these skills.

These skills training 'packages' stress three main phases of skilled counsellor activity: to facilitate exploration, understanding and action. They thus all have their roots in the client-centred tradition but in their different ways have added other phases and skills not emphasised by this approach. As mentioned above, they all tried to break down broad counselling processes into teachable and learnable skills, although they vary concerning the degree to which they specify these skills (see Larson, 1984; Baker, Daniels and Greeley, 1990, for a fuller discussion of these and other skills training 'packages').

Before describing how such skills may be taught, some advantages and disadvantages of skills training will be considered. If skills training is considered as one interdependent part of the entire training process, then it can be a very useful way of encouraging trainees (1) to distinguish between helpful and unhelpful ways of responding to clients and (2) to make helpful responses in a clear and effective manner. However, if skills training is seen as the only approach to counsellor education or if it is given undue importance in the curriculum, then there is a danger that trainees may become good technicians without having the opportunity to examine their attitudes towards themselves, others and the world. Thus, the relationship between skills training and self-exploration work, in particular, is a delicate one which needs careful monitoring. The object is neither to train good but unaware technicians, nor to train aware but poor communicators. Both endeavours are important and are intertwined.

If the view is taken that breaking down broad descriptions of effective counselling into more discrete counselling skills is a worthwhile activity* and that these skills can be taught and learned, then *how* can this be done?

Carkhuff (1969) made the important point that there are two major elements to effective counsellor communication. The first involves good discrimination skills, i.e. trainee counsellors need to be able to discriminate (1) between accurate and inaccurate formulations of what clients communicate and (2) between helpful and unhelpful counsellor responses

---

*Not all counsellor trainers take this view. In particular, psychodynamic trainers tend to place less emphasis on skills training, focusing more on the blocks to effective communication.

to these communications. Thus, before being able to respond effectively to clients, trainees need to be accurate in their understanding of what their clients are experiencing and what might constitute helpful responses to this experiencing. Exercises designed to sharpen trainees' discrimination skills include the presentation of client statements either on audio, video or in written form, along with a number of options which detail (1) accurate and inaccurate representations of the client's experience and, later, (2) helpful and unhelpful counsellor responses (with respect to the target skill) to that experience. Trainees then have to choose an option that best represents the client's experience and the most helpful counsellor response. Discussion follows that usually centres on the basis for the trainees' choices.

When trainees demonstrate adequate discrimination on a particular skill, the emphasis shifts to the second major element – namely effective responding in using the target skill.

Methods

The following outlines a typical sequence of counselling skills training.

1. A discussion of helpful vs unhelpful skills. Here it is advisable to provide a conceptual framework, like the one indicated by Egan (1990), at the outset of training so that trainees can be helped to make sense of the entire counselling process and helped to see where and when particular skills fit into the overall structure.
2. A discussion of the purpose of particular skills, noting that different counselling skills can be used for different purposes. For example, some skills (e.g. open-ended questions) are used to widen the scope of the client's exploration, whereas other skills (e.g. summarising) are designed to focus the client's exploration.
3. The trainer models the skill to be learned by role-playing a counselling session with a 'client' or by actually counselling a trainee in front of the training group.
4. Trainees are then encouraged to practise skills by role-play or co-counselling.
5. Trainees are given feed-back on their skills by the trainer and/or by fellow observing trainees. Most counsellor trainers acknowledge the importance of focusing on the experience of the person in the 'client' role at this particular point so that the impact of such skills on the client can be evaluated. Where appropriate and where feasible, the use of audiovisual technology can be employed to facilitate this learning process.

It is not known, however, exactly how concretely counsellor trainers specify the skill to be learned. Taking empathic responding as an example, it is possible to teach trainees to make specific concrete empathic responses or to operate in an empathic mode where the trainee related to the 'client' according to the general principle: respond to the client from the latter's internal frame of reference. Trainees are likely to receive feedback of varying specificity according to the nature of the training offered.

Theory and Academic Work

Counselling theory and related academic work is all too frequently the poor relation on counselling courses. Many trainees have vivid past memories of sitting passively while academics deliver lectures on topics that could easily be read in books. In the previous chapter the case was made for this element of counselling training. It should be noted here that how it is approached often determines the degree to which trainees value theoretical and academic material.

Lectures

Counselling trainees, in general, will not tolerate a course where lectures are the predominant way in which knowledge is communicated; also they should not have to do so. However, lectures do have their place on a counselling course. They should be given to outline a framework within which subsequent theoretical/academic material can best be understood. Also, well-delivered lectures on topics not easily accessible in written form are usually well appreciated by students. In both these cases, however, the lecturer should give trainees plenty of time to discuss and ask questions about the presented material.

Seminars

When academic material is easily accessible in written form, seminars can be usefully held to discuss matters arising from this material. The success of these seminars depends upon (1) trainees undertaking to read the material before the seminar is held; (2) a list of discussion items being presented well in advance of the seminar; and (3) someone, either a tutor or trainee, leading the discussion in a focused way and encouraging participants to keep to the theme of the seminar. On this latter point, if trainees are to lead effective seminars they will need guidance on how they can best do so; otherwise trainee-led seminars can easily degenerate into lectures given by the trainee. This also happens when fellow trainees have not read the material in advance. To prevent this from happening, readings need to be focused and manageable, given the constraints of time and the other demands that the course places on trainees. On some courses, learning contracts are made which specify what trainees agree to read and, as long as the amount of reading is manageable, these contracts can be effective. However, unless the contracts are made in a spirit of negotiation, trainees may experience them as coercive.

The size of the seminar group is another important variable in determining the success of seminars: 13–14 trainees is the absolute maximum number for a seminar group where productive debate and discussion can take place and groups of 8 or 9 are preferable.

Tutorials

In the current climate of deteriorating staff–student ratios, it is unlikely that courses in institutions of further and higher education will be able to offer students regular individual or small group academic tutorials. This is a pity because this approach to academic work can be very stimulating for both tutor and trainee. At a minimum, however, each trainee should have one individual tutorial per term in which the trainee's academic development is discussed along with his or her progress in the three other elements discussed in this chapter.

Projects

Much useful collaborative academic work can be carried out by a group of trainees electing to study a particular area or facet of counselling, to prepare the material and to present this to the rest of the course. This approach is particularly well utilised by courses that are organised around the principle of self-directed learning.

Whichever teaching or learning methods are used, however, academic work should not be isolated from the rest of the curriculum and previous remarks concerning the interrelated nature of the four elements discussed in this chapter bear one final reiteration.

References

AVELINE, M.O. (1990). The training and supervision of individual therapists. In W. Dryden (Ed.), *Individual Therapy: A handbook*. Milton Keynes: Open University Press.

BAKER, S.B., DANIELS T.G. and GREELEY, A. (1990). Systematic training of graduate-level counselors: Narrative and meta-analytic reviews of three major programs. *The Counseling Psychologist*, **18**, 355–421.

BEUTLER, L.E., CRAGO, M. and ARIZMENDI, T.G. (1986). Research on therapist variables in psychotherapy. In S.L. Garfield and A.E. Bergin (Eds), *Handbook of Psychotherapy and Behavior Change*, 3rd edn. New York: Wiley.

CARKHUFF, R.R. (1969). *Helping and Human Relations: A primer for lay and professional helpers*, vols 1 and 2. New York: Rinehart & Winston.

CARKHUFF R.R. (1987). *The Art of Helping VI*. Amherst, MA: Human Resource Development Press.

COVNER, B.J. (1944). Studies in phonographic recordings of verbal material: III. The completeness and accuracy of counselling interview reports. *Journal of General Psychology*, **30**, 181–203.

DRYDEN, W. (Ed.). (1984). *Individual Therapy in Britain.* Milton Keynes: Open University Press.

DRYDEN, W. (1987). *Current Issues in Rational–Emotive Therapy.* Beckenham, Kent: Croom Helm.

DRYDEN, W. (1989). The therapeutic alliance as an integrating framework. In W. Dryden (Ed.), *Key Issues for Counselling in Action.* London: Sage.

DRYDEN, W. (1990). *Dryden on Counselling. Volume 1: Seminal papers.* London: Whurr Publishers.

EGAN, G. (1990). *The Skilled Helper: A systematic approach to effective helping,* 4th edn. Pacific Grove, CA: Brooks/Cole.

ELLIOTT, R. and SHAPIRO, D.A. (1988). Brief structured recall: A more efficient method for studying significant therapy events. *British Journal of Medical Psychology,* **61**, 141–153.

EVISON, R. and HOROBIN, R. (1988). Co-counselling. In: J. Rowan and W. Dryden (Eds), *Innovative Therapy in Britain.* Milton Keynes: Open University Press.

HILL, C.E. and O'GRADY, K.E. (1985). List of therapist intentions illustrated in a case study and with therapists of varying theoretical orientations. *Journal of Counseling Psychology,* **32**, 3–22.

IVEY, A.E. (1988). *Intentional Interviewing and Counseling: Facilitating client development.* Pacific Grove, CA: Brooks/Cole.

JACOBS, M. (1981). Setting the record straight. *Counselling,* No. 36, 10–13.

JACOBS, M. (1988). *The Presenting Past.* London: Harper & Row.

KAGAN, N. (1984). Interpersonal process recall: Basic methods and recent research. In: D Larson (Ed.). *Teaching Psychological Skills: Models for giving psychology away.* Monterey, CA: Brooks/Cole.

KAGAN, N. and KAGAN, H. (1990). IPR: A validated model for the 1990s and beyond. *The Counseling Psychologist,* **18**, 436–440.

LARSON, D. (Ed.) (1984). *Teaching Psychological Skills: Models for giving psychology away.* Monterey, CA: Brooks/Cole.

MUSLIN, H.L., THURNBLAD, R.J. and MESCHEL, G. (1981). The fate of the clinical interview: An observational study. *American Journal of Psychiatry,* **138** (6), 825–833.

MCNEILL, B.W. and WORTHEN, V. (1989). The parallel process in psychotherapy supervision. *Professional Psychology: Research and Practice,* **20**, 329–333.

PROGOFF, I. (1975). *At a Journal Workshop.* New York: Dialogue House Library.

TRUAX, C.B. and CARKHUFF, R.R. (1967). *Toward Effective Counseling and Psychotherapy: Training and practice.* Chicago: Aldine.

Chapter 3
Teaching Counselling Skills to Non-psychologists

This chapter was first published by invitation in the *British Journal of Medical Psychology* (1985) as part of a symposium entitled 'Sharing psychological skills'. I used the opportunity to consider the nature of counselling skills, where and how such skills can be taught and to whom, and the tricky question of the effectiveness of counselling skills training approaches. In part the chapter was based on the experiences of a number of counselling skills trainers working in medical settings whom I interviewed while preparing material for the chapter. The chapter here has been expanded so that methods of counselling skills training could be discussed in greater detail.

The purpose of this chapter is to outline issues involved in teaching counselling skills to non-psychologists, with reference to medical and paramedical personnel. It should be noted at the outset that, despite the fact that both a national organisation for the advancement of counselling in Britain (the British Association for Counselling) and a special group for counselling psychology within the British Psychological Society exist, there is little centralised information concerning the nature and extent of counselling skills training for medical and paramedical personnel. What work is being carried out apart from that of Peter Maguire and his colleagues in Manchester (Maguire et al., 1980, 1983), is largely unresearched. Thus, it appears that there is considerable scope for innovative research-based work in this field in Britain. As there is little centralised information on this topic, I interviewed a random sample of leading British trainers who regularly teach counselling skills to medical and paramedical staff. Their views on the themes of the paper were elicited and have helped to form the basis of this chapter (see Acknowledgements).

The Nature of Counselling Skills

Counselling has been defined by the British Association of Counselling as follows:

> People become engaged in counselling when a person, occupying *regularly* or *temporarily* the role of counsellor offers or agrees explicitly to offer *time, attention* and *respect* to another person or persons temporarily in the role of client. The task of counselling is to give the client an opportunity to *explore, discover and clarify* ways of *living* more resourcefully and toward greater well-being.

Implicit in this definition are a number of issues that will be covered in this chapter, namely (1) counselling can be carried out formally and/or informally; (2) counselling involves important attitudes and skills on the part of the helper; and (3) the nature of the counsellor's task changes over time.

Rogers (1957) has cogently argued that the nature of successful counselling involves the counsellor communicating core attitudinal conditions to the client. These 'core conditions' are empathy, unconditional acceptance and genuineness. Successful counselling is deemed to occur when the client actually perceives and experiences these conditions. Counsellor training, both in Britain and North America, has continued to be heavily influenced by the work of Rogers, despite the fact that recent research has cast doubt on the relationship of the 'core conditions' and successful outcome (Mitchell, Bozarth and Krauft, 1977). Kurtz and Marshall (1982) note that since the advent of Rogers' pioneering work in the late 1950s and 1960s, the history of training counsellors has moved 'from qualitative helper attitudes to discrete behavioural units; from core conditions for facilitating the helping relationship to a broad range of skills for performing numerous helper activities. . .; from purely didactic or experiential training paradigms to training approaches that combine both; and from person- or trainee-centred programmes to skills-centred curricula' (p. 9).

There exist numerous training packages, developed almost exclusively in the USA, which British counsellor trainers can use. An exception to this is the work of John Heron (1976) who pioneered a 'six category intervention analysis' training scheme. These categories fall into two groups:

1. Authoritative, which includes prescriptive, informative and confronting interventions.
2. Facilitative, which includes cathartic, catalytic and supportive interventions.

However, Heron's scheme has not been widely used in Britain. More widely practised is Egan's (1975, 1990) model. As such it will be used here to illustrate what core skills tend to be taught to people interested in adopting the role of counsellor, informally or formally, as part of their work. The popularity of Egan's model has been enhanced by recent visits of Gerard Egan to Britain and by its use as the basis of two BBC radio programmes entitled *'Principles of Counselling*: Series 1 and 2' Egan's model is eclectic in that it advocates the use of different stages in the helping process, and at each stage the counsellor has a different fundamental task.

In stage 1, the counsellor's major task is to encourage the client to engage in affective self-exploration. Here the core counselling skills are: verbal and non-verbal attending behaviour; active listening to the client's verbal and non-verbal messages; responding to the client from the latter's internal frame of reference (reflection of feeling and content is particularly appropriate here); and the constructive use of probing to encourage clients to be more concrete in their self-exploration. Training at this level is focused on helping trainees to perceive clients' messages accurately and to respond appropriately to these messages so that clients are encouraged to explore themselves and their phenomenal world more deeply than they are able at the beginning of the counselling process.

The major task of the counsellor in stage 2 of Egan's model is to promote dynamic self-understanding (where clients are helped to view themselves and their life situations from new, more constructive perspectives) and the preliminary establishment of action-based goals. First, the core skill of summarising is used. Here, the counsellor helps the client to identify recurring themes that have been expressed during the initial period of self-exploration. This sets the scene for the core skill of appropriate challenging to be used. The purpose of such challenges is to enable the client to see things from an alternative, wider and more constructive perspective. Appropriate challenges may be made in a number of ways. First, the counsellor may offer advanced accurate empathy; here hunches are tentatively shared concerning the self-defeating manner in which the client has been living his or her life. These hunches are formed from what the client has implicitly expressed. Secondly, the counsellor may confront the client concerning the nature of these self-defeating patterns. Thirdly, self-disclosure may be employed; here the counsellor shares some relevant aspect of his or her life to provide the client with possible alternative ways of coping. Fourthly, immediacy may be fostered; here, the counsellor encourages the client to consider his or her own relationship as an example of how the client may defeat him- or herself by making faulty assumptions about the nature of that relationship. This leads to a discussion of how the client can extricate him- or herself from such self-defeating patterns. The counsellor also employs these challenging skills to help the client to begin to set goals for acting and living his or her life in a different, more constructive manner.

The third major task of the counsellor, according to this model, is to promote constructive action. Here, the counsellor helps the client to identify a variety of possibilities for acting differently, to evaluate these different possibilities and to choose appropriate action plans. In short, the client is helped to set goals based on dynamic self-understanding. The client is then helped to implement such plans and, thence, to evaluate their outcomes.

It is clear from this description that, in order for these skills to be adequately learned and mastered, an ongoing period of training should be offered which ideally would involve providing trainees with feed-back on their actual counselling work with clients. In reality, in Britain, most training schemes for medical and paramedical personnel are short term in nature and, as a result, the focus is largely restricted to the stage 1 skills of encouraging the client to engage in affective self-exploration. For example, some health authorities send medical and paramedical staff on short (3- or 5-day) training courses. These courses may be residential or non-residential (e.g. Faulkner and Nurse, 1981). An exception is the 6-month training programme offered by the Royal College of Nursing which endeavours to teach trainees the core skills in each of the three stages mentioned above.

An important issue emerges in skills-based counsellor training pro-grammes. To what extent does such training, by itself, enable trainees to acquire the appropriate facilitative attitudes or should other training experience be added? Most of the trainers interviewed considered that skills-based training does have some positive impact on the development of constructive counsellor attitudes, but conceded that an additional period of trainee self-exploration is needed within a setting where personal development is specifically encouraged. There is little existing research to shed light on this important issue.

Framework

Skills-based counsellor training such as that outlined above assumes that: (1) such skills can be taught and learned; (2) such learning is best fostered when trainers offer trainees the same 'core-conditions' as counsellors offer their clients; (3) relevant skills can be demonstrated by trainers, practised by trainees in simulated exercises and refined by constructive feed-back. Thus skills-based training is based on a humanistic–behavioural model of human functioning which emphasises *both* a constructive learning environment *and* detailed instruction as necessary for the acquisition of counselling skills. It parallels the model of counselling implicit in Egan's schema, where again the provision of both 'core conditions' and skill training is deemed to be necessary for constructive client growth.

The model of training outlined here also assumes that: (1) counselling skills, thus acquired, can then be demonstrated by medical and paramedi-cal practitioners in their actual work setting; and (2) the demonstration of such skills will make a significant difference to the client's well-being.

However, this 'training–demonstration–impact' model still awaits empirical inquiry. Another assumption made by the counselling skills model is that these skills can in fact be acquired by most people. Other trainers believe that you cannot make a 'silk purse out of a sow's ear' and a level of intuitive feeling for other people should be present in potential trainees before training is offered.

The relationship between trainers and trainees in the skills-based model also parallels the relationship between counsellor and client in that, in both settings, trainer/counsellor and trainee/client are deemed to have an egalitarian relationship, albeit where the trainer may have a greater level of experience in pertinent areas.

Who is to be Taught?

One answer to this question is that all medical and paramedical personnel should be trained in counselling skills. Although they may not wish to adopt a specific counselling role, the skills that they will acquire from such training will be of use to them in helping to form more constructive relationships with their patients and colleagues. Indeed, particularly in North America, and increasingly now in Britain, a vast majority of medical students are given skills-based instruction in the related area of interpersonal skills training. However, Gaynor Nurse (personal communication) has suggested that such training should be available but optional, so that people can determine for themselves whether they, in fact, wish to adopt a counselling role.

Another related issue concerns whether such training should only be available for people who are trained medical or paramedical practitioners or available more widely to include those still in training. The opinions of trainers interviewed differed on this point; on the one hand, the view was expressed that such training should be offered from the beginning of a student's medical career in order to help him or her to focus on the more humane aspects of their role. On the other hand, it was considered that 18–21 year olds have enough to cope with digesting the vast amount of knowledge that they have to acquire as part of their training; thus they would not be ready to engage in the painful process of self-exploration which often accompanies training in counselling skills.

Methods

Among the trainers who were interviewed and who are actively engaged in teaching counselling skills to medical and paramedical personnel, there was a reasonable consensus concerning the methods that are actually involved in such training, although no single trainer employed all such methods. The following elements are regularly found in skills-based counsellor training schemes: (1) instruction; (2) modelling; (3) practice; and (4) feed-back (Ford, 1979). I will now briefly consider each in turn and will assume that skills are to be taught one at a time.

Instruction

Instruction is used throughout the skills training process but is particularly salient at the outset in both a general and specific sense. In the general sense, at the beginning of a skills training group the tutor will explain verbally, and with reference to handouts and set texts, the overall model of skills training to be employed during this component of the training course. This model may be one already in existence, an amalgam of what is available or one devised by the tutor. Whichever approach is used, it is important that trainees are given an overall picture of the model and its purpose, and have an opportunity to discuss it before specific skills are introduced.

When specific skills are introduced, instructions (where the skill is explained and its purpose and limits thoroughly discussed) are helpful before modelling is introduced.

Modelling

After a skill has been introduced and explained many tutors (but not all) present a good model of the skill to be learned. Ford (1979) notes that there are three issues with respect to this modelling: (1) the model, (2) the message and (3) the medium.

With respect to the *model* it is likely that a coping model (i.e. good enough but not perfect) is more helpful than one which shows flawless performance (the mastery model) in encouraging trainees to practise the skill with confidence. Mastery models can lead trainees to feel hopeless about learning the skill whilst coping models are more credible for trainees and tend to inspire hope. It is for this reason that flawless live performances by tutors and by master counsellors on video tape have their limitations as effective models at least until trainees have internalised the target skill.

With respect to the *message*, it is important, as noted above, that demonstration of effective *and* ineffective examples of the skill be modelled so that trainees can learn to discriminate accurately before being expected to respond effectively. If audio or video models are portrayed, relevant cues (e.g. audible tones or captions) need to be used if trainees are to be helped to recognise the skill, especially if it is embedded in counselling interactions where other skills may be demonstrated.

With respect to the *medium*, models can be live, shown on video tape, heard on audio tape or presented in written form. Obviously the target skill will determine to a large extent the medium used (e.g. non-verbal skills require live or video-taped demonstration).

Earlier it was mentioned that not all tutors use modelling at this stage of the skills training process. Such tutors fear that exposure to models at this point might lead trainees to imitate the model rather than integrate the skill into their natural style of responding. Thus, such tutors proceed directly from instruction to practice and use modelling at a later stage of the counselling skills training process to demonstrate the range of ways of implementing these skills.

Practice

When trainees are given an opportunity to practise the skill under consideration, there are different ways in which this can be done. Perhaps the most frequently used approach is to use 'peer counselling' where one trainee counsels a fellow trainee for a period of time. The question which then arises concerns whether the trainee client discusses a real concern or adopts the role of a client and invents a problem. The main advantage of the 'real problem' situation is that the 'client' is referring to his or her own real feelings during the counselling and can give reliable feed-back to the counsellor concerning the impact of the skill under consideration. Also the 'client' can be successfully helped to explore a significant issue by the peer 'counsellor', showing them both that trainees can be helpful in the counselling role. The main disadvantage is that the client may go further in his or her exploration of the concern than anticipated and become quite distressed as a result. In such cases, the amount and quality of support present on the course is a crucial factor in determining the impact of this situation on the distressed trainee. In many respects, trainers are responsible for creating a 'holding' environment for their trainees. An obvious but sometimes neglected maxim here is 'put the welfare of the trainee before skills practice' if the two conflict. However, if the skills group is the only forum in which trainees can explore themselves, this blurring of the boundaries is inevitable with dubious results. In such cases, trainees will have neither sufficient time for learning skills nor adequate opportunity to explore concerns in depth and at length.

The disadvantage of role-playing a client in skills practice is that the 'client' can either abandon the role in an attempt to be a 'good' client for his or her colleague or may stick rigidly to the role, negating any helpful shift in experience as a result of counselling. It is a skill in itself to portray accurately a role with the right degree of flexibility. This is why some courses employ actors on occasion to play the role of clients. However, the main advantage of role-playing is that it not only safeguards the welfare of trainees but later in the course the 'client' trainee can play the role of his or her own clients and learn more about the latter, sometimes with great immediacy.

Other approaches to skills practice involve responding to brief written audio-taped or video-taped 'client' vignettes and the use of actors (as noted above). Rarely, if ever, are genuine clients used in counselling skills groups.

Feed-back

Trainees will best learn and refine their counselling skills if they are given feed-back. Ford (1979) has noted that there are four issues with respect to feed-back: (1) the message; (2) feed-back valence; (3) the medium; and (4) the source.

With respect to the *message*, feed-back may be a simple 'right' or 'wrong' response or it may include information which (1) encourages greater discrimination, (2) provides greater explanation than had been given hitherto and (3) involves the use of modelling. The main research finding concerning the message component of feed-back is that performance-specific feed-back is more effective than non-specific feed-back in aiding the acquisition of the target counselling skill (Ford, 1979).

The *valence* of the feed-back ranges from positive to negative in kind or more neutral informational feed-back. It is the experience of most trainers that judiciously given positive feed-back, with specific information and instructions concerning future improvement, is the type found most useful by trainees, although this area needs to be researched. Consistent negative feed-back is destructive and demoralising, consistent positive feed-back has a pollyannaish quality to it which leads trainees to doubt the sincerity of the feed-back source, whilst consistent neutral (informational) feed-back leaves trainees wondering about how well or poorly they are performing.

Concerning the *medium* of feed-back, this is usually verbal, although written feed-back is also used by tutors in interim or final evaluations of trainee performance in skills groups. The use of numerical feed-back is also appropriate if the tutor is using scales (such as Carkhuff's (1969) five-point scales of counsellor functioning) to indicate a range of skill levels.

Also, if feed-back is to be given, the source of the feed-back needs direct access to skill performance. One way is through live observation. Here feed-back can be given at the end of an observed sequence, or during it (either through the use of bug-in-the-ear devices or when the source interrupts the sequence to make a point). How and when feed-back is given in this respect can vary according to the trainee's preference.

Feed-back can also be given in response to audio-taped or video-taped counselling sessions, video being particularly useful when non-verbal skills are salient. However, trainees will need to become comfortable using these media while counselling before benefiting fully from such feed-back.

Finally, the *source* of the feed-back can be the tutor, the trainee client, an observer (if counselling triads are used) or the trainee counsellor who gives feed-back to him- or herself. All four are best used in rotation unless this becomes confusing for the trainee. If only tutor feed-back is given, this communicates that trainees' views are unimportant, whilst if only trainees' feed-back is used the expertise of the tutor is not utilised. Here, as elsewhere in counsellor training (see Chapter 2), a healthy balance should be the objective.

Before leaving this discussion of skills training, it needs to be stressed that other methods can be used to add a useful dimension to the emphasis on skills. Thus interpersonal process recall (IPR) methods (Kagan and Kagan, 1990) can be very helpful during skills training to elucidate the covert and often difficult to identify elements of 'counsellor' or 'client' experience, e.g. during skills practice sessions. Here the tutor (or someone else) replays the tape of the counselling, encouraging 'counsellor' or 'client' to stop the tape whenever they want to discuss an important experience felt during the counselling and recalled by listening to the tape. This experiential element often sheds light on the session which might otherwise be neglected due to the emphasis on observable skills. Whilst IPR should not be used exclusively in skills training because it was not designed to facilitate skill acquisition (Kagan and Kagan, 1990), it can be usefully employed as an adjunct in skills training to tease out relevant covert experiences which need to be processed *along with* the focus on observable skills.

The focus here has been on the acquisition of discrete skills. Similar remarks can be made concerning how integration of skills can be approached, although this is a complex issue and beyond the scope of this chapter. Suffice it to say, the development of skill integration is a slow process in which supervision of casework plays a central role (see Chapters 2 and 4).

Where?

The counsellor trainers who were interviewed tended to differ concerning where training should be held. Some favoured in-service training in the hospital where trainees worked, the familiar surroundings helping to facilitate the generalisation of skills, whilst other trainers considered it important for trainees to receive training away from their place of work, often attending residential programmes. I formed the impression that the latter group tended to stress the importance of trainee self-exploration as an integral part of the training process more than the former group. One trainer mentioned that if trainees wished to develop the counselling aspects of their work role, then it was important for them to join counselling courses where they could meet and work with counsellors from other settings so that their perspective on counselling could be widened and their exploration enriched by working with people who have other areas of expertise.

Effectiveness

One of the disappointing aspects of counsellor training in Britain is that there has been little empirical work carried out on its effectiveness. This is true whether the focus is on the immediate acquisition of such skills by trainees (to what extent does skills-based training help trainees acquire such skills?), on the retention of new skills (if skills are acquired, to what extent are they retained in the person's response repertoire?) or on the impact that retained and demonstrated skills have on the client's well-being. Whilst a number of North American studies have demonstrated that trainees can acquire such skills in the short term (e.g. Robbins et al., 1979), the long-term effects of such training have been relatively unexplored and where they have been studied the outcome has not been generally optimistic (e.g. Kauss et al., 1980). It seems that, in general, trainees can acquire counselling skills but require frequent refresher courses to maintain them.

Peter Maguire and his colleagues have endeavoured to research their work and have some interesting data concerning the impact of demonstrable counselling skills on client well-being. They have shown that a trained counsellor can have significant positive impact on the degree of social recovery, reintegration into work and adaptation to breast loss with mastectomy patients, although counselling seemed to have little impact on the degree of physical disability of these patients (Maguire et al., 1983). An earlier study (Maguire et al., 1980) showed that, whilst counsellors/nurses did not have a direct impact on the psychiatric morbidity of patients, they were helpful in recognising the early signs of psychiatric disturbance and effecting an appropriate referral, with the result that the level of psychiatric morbidity among mastectomy patients receiving counselling was less than those who did not receive counselling. Given the dearth of empirical studies in Britain on the impact of training on counsellor functioning and on patient well-being, it is suggested that specific studies for specific conditions, such as the one carried out by Maguire, be pursued in depth. Researchers can then by-pass such problematic questions as: 'Does counselling really work?'; 'Is counselling skills training effective?' and deal with more manageable questions such as 'Which counselling skills are effective for which group of patients at which stage in treatment?'; and 'Which method of counselling skills training is effective with which trainees at which stage in training?'

A number of areas of empirical inquiry have already been noted, but one particular hypothesis needs to be tested. This states that the degree to which trainees are able to demonstrate both a high level of facilitative attitudes and associated skill in the counselling setting will be positively correlated with the degree to which they have had an opportunity to focus specifically on and change self-defeating attitudes and beliefs which might interfere with their work in a counselling role.

Conclusion

It is apparent that the teaching of counselling skills to medical and paramedical personnel is very much in its infancy in Britain and many more questions are forthcoming than answers available, namely, with regard to the nature of counsellor training:

1. To what extent should such training focus exclusively on skills or should an approach which encourages trainees to focus on themselves be included?
2. To what extent does the role of informal or formal counselling, which is rooted in the philosophy of patient-centred care, conflict with task-centred medical care?
3. To what extent does the ethos of medical training with its emphasis on competence, expertness and strength conflict with the counselling ethos of acknowledging weaknesses, anxieties and doubts, and acknowledging an egalitarian role with clients?

Returning to more parochial matters, such questions arise as the following:

1. To what extent should counselling be on the curriculum at all?
2. If included, to what extent should counselling be a mandatory or an optional part of a training curriculum?
3. Should medical personnel be offered the opportunity to adopt an informal counselling role or to what extent should it be considered a mandatory part of their role?
4. If medical personnel are going to be trained in counselling skills in any systematic way, how much support (and thereby financial resources) should be given to these people as they undertake the arduous task of learning to become counsellors?

Whilst there are no ready answers to these questions, some of them are dependent on individual philosophy of health care and how that person would like to see the National Health Service in Britain develop. Others can be answered by empirical inquiry and it is hoped that British researchers will increasingly turn their attention to this under-researched area. (Since this was written, Hilton Davis and his colleagues have been and continue to be active researchers in this area.)

Acknowledgements

I am grateful to the following people for their views on counsellor training in medical settings: John Heron, Janet Lake, Gaynor Nurse and Bill Stewart. I also wish to thank Tim Betts, John Heron, Peter Maguire, Gaynor Nurse and Bill Stewart for providing me with valuable resource material.

References

CARKHUFF, R.R. (1969). *Helping and Human Relations*, vols 1 and 2. New York: Holt, Rinehart & Winston.

EGAN, G. (1975). *The Skilled Helper: A model for systematic helping and interpersonal relating.* Monterey, CA: Brooks/Cole.

EGAN, G. (1990). *The Skilled Helper: A systematic approach to effective helping,* 4th edn. Pacific Grove, CA: Brooks/Cole.

FAULKNER, A. and NURSE, G. (1981). Counselling patients with cancer. *Nursing Focus,* April, 268–269.

FORD, J.D. (1979). Research on training counselors and clinicians. *Review of Educational Research,* **49,** 87–130.

HERON, J. (1976). A six category intervention analysis. *British Journal of Guidance and Counselling,* **4,** 143–155.

KAGAN, N. and KAGAN, H. (1990). IPR: A validated model for the 1990s and beyond. *The Counseling Psychologist,* **18,** 436–440.

KAUSS, D.R., ROBBINS, A.S., ABRASS, I., BAKAITIS, R.F. and ANDERSON, L.A. (1980). The long-term effectiveness of interpersonal skills training in medical schools. *Journal of Medical Education,* **55,** 595–601.

KURTZ, P.B. and MARSHALL, E.K. (1982). Evolution of interpersonal skills training. In: E.K. Marshall, P.B. Kurtz and Associates (Eds), *Interpersonal Helping Skills: A guide to training methods, programs, and resources.* San Francisco, CA: Jossey-Bass.

MAGUIRE, P., TAIT, A., BROOKE, M., THOMAS, C. and SELLWOOD, R. (1980). Effect of counselling on the psychiatric morbidity associated with mastectomy. *British Medical Journal,* **281,** 1454–1456.

MAGUIRE, P., BROOKE, M., TAIT, A., THOMAS, C. and SELLWOOD, R. (1983). The effect of counselling on physical disability and social recovery after mastectomy. *Clinical Oncology,* **9,** 319–324.

MITCHELL, K.M., BOZARTH, J.D. and KRAUFT, C.C. (1977). A reappraisal of the therapeutic effectiveness of accurate empathy, nonpossessive warmth and genuineness. In: A.S. Gurman and A.M. Razin (Eds), *Effective Psychotherapy.* New York: Pergamon.

ROBBINS, A.S., KAUSS, D.R., HEINRICH, R., ABRASS, I., DREYER, J. and CLYMAN, B. (1979). Interpersonal skills training: Evaluation in an internal medicine residency. *Journal of Medical Education,* **54,** 885–894.

ROGERS, C.R. (1957). The necessary and sufficient conditions of therapeutic personality change. *Journal of Consulting Psychology,* **21,** 95–103.

Chapter 4
The Importance of Case Discussion in Counsellor Training

In this early paper (published in 1977) I consider the role of case discussion in counsellor training. I argue that it is the best forum to promote trainees' understanding of their cases and, when used in conjunction with supervision of audio tapes of their counselling work, it is a powerful approach to training counsellors. The paper was written at an interesting time in my development as a counsellor and counsellor trainer. It was when I was ending my experimentation with psychodynamic methods of counselling and beginning to become interested in rational–emotive counselling. Consequently, whilst I still consider case discussion to be an important training medium, I would no longer go along with some of the psychodynamically inspired insights I made in the paper.

Over the last two decades, an increasing number of books have emphasised the technological aspects of counsellor training (e.g. Ivey, 1971, 1988; Egan, 1975, 1990). These books have stressed that counselling is a skill that can be broken down into subskills. Whilst such a view has its value, it can be taken too far in the training process, leading to the creation of the counsellor-technologist. The danger here has been pointed out by Patterson (1977), who has expressed his fear that in their quest to be increasingly innovative, counsellor-technologists are tending to lose sight of (or deny) a very important part of the counselling process, i.e. the therapeutic relationship between counsellor and client.

It is the basic thesis of this chapter that any training scheme which does not stress the importance of 'therapeutic understanding', as well as skills development, will in the long run be unsuccessful. The counsellor is not a dispenser of accurate empathy or genuineness, but 'a person who allows himself to be discovered as a genuine person who cares about his client and knows in experience how he feels' (Hazell, 1974).

When counsellor trainers wish to focus on trainees' counselling skills development, then skills training is the appropriate approach. However, when trainers want to enhance trainees' understanding of their clients, then they need to use case discussion to help trainees to understand themselves within the context of the counselling relationship. Accordingly, case discussion is regarded as being an important component of the counsellor training process (see also Chapter 2).

Before trainees see clients, however, they should be able to display a minimal level of accurate empathy (as measured by Carkhuff's (1969) five-point Empathic Understanding Scale). Thus they are shown the value of responding to the client from the latter's frame of reference, in a way which does not detract from the affect and meaning communicated by the client. To this end the skill-building approaches of Ivey (1988) and Egan (1990) are useful: the subskills of accurate understanding of concept and emotion are identified, practised and shaped in dyadic role-play, after which the 'counsellor' is given feed-back from both the trainer and the other trainees (see Chapter 3). However, once trainees begin to see clients, the emphasis on skill technology can be reduced (identifying and practising the 'skills' of genuineness, confrontation, self-disclosure, and immediacy are difficult, since the therapeutic value of making such responses is heavily dependent on 'client' and 'context' variables), and the emphasis on 'therapeutic understanding' increased. At this stage, case discussion assumes greater importance as a training mode, and takes place in two settings: individual supervision and the seminar group. In both, use can be made of tape recordings that trainees have made of their counselling interviews.

Individual Supervision

In individual supervision, the trainee is asked to introduce the case by telling his or her supervisor a little about the client and how — in his or her opinion — the interview progressed. As Bruch (1974) has pointed out, the tape recorder should not be considered a replacement for the verbal report of the trainee's perceptions of what transpired in the interview, since this report will provide the supervisor with a line of inquiry. Often I am struck either by a pattern in what the trainee has been saying or has not been saying, or by the tone of voice the trainee uses in talking about the case. After exploration of the issues that emerge, we listen to a tape segment which is relevant to the discussion. Here our attention may be directed to specific responses: for example, 'How might you have phrased that remark in a way which would enable the client to see how sad he was feeling?'. Trainees have, however, found that focusing on response (micro-level analysis) is far more valuable after they have had some opportunity to explore with their supervisor the dynamics of the relationship (macro-level analysis) than before such exploration. Gendlin (1964) has made a similar point with regard to client insight: a client may acknowledge that he gets angry whenever his mother asks him about his work, but such acknowledgement has much more therapeutic value after he has had an opportunity to explore the personal meanings that the mother's question holds for him.

Rogers and Truax (1967) have stressed how important it is for the counsellor to be sensitive to the moment-by-moment changes in clients' statements, and it is my experience that trainees are less sensitive to clients' expressions of their resources than they are to clients' expressions of their weaknesses, i.e. they focus predominantly on 'problem' material. It is in the individual supervision sessions that such micro-level matters can be explored. It is, however, equally important for the trainee to be aware of the client's preferred style of functioning and of the relationship at a more global level. This macro-level form of analysis is more valuably undertaken in the group seminars.

The Seminar Group

The aim in the group seminar sessions is to help the trainee to 'get in touch with the covert processes that are always going on between a therapist and his client, no matter what the theoretical orientation may be' (Rioch, Coulter and Weinberger, 1976, p.8). Again the trainee is asked to present a case, but this time she is invited to formulate a question which she wants the group to consider and on which she wants to be helped towards an answer. Often the trainee presents a case that is not going too well, and the question indicates that the counsellor and her client have come to an impasse in their relationship. After the trainee has presented the case and posed her question, the group is encouraged to help her explore the issues involved.

I have been struck by the frequency with which the ensuing exploration leads to the realisation that the trainee is struggling with feelings which she should not have, e.g. boredom, anger, frustration, hopelessness. Trainees usually hold two implicit but related assumptions about their counselling practice: that they must be competent, and that they must feel warm towards their clients. Thus, whenever they consider that they have made a 'bad response' or are feeling anything but warmth for their client, they are unable to use their feelings as a possible guide to understanding the client, and consequently an impasse in their relationship is reached.

In this situation, the group aided by the trainer can help the trainee to see that there are more therapeutic ways of using her feelings in the relationship. The trainee can be encouraged to entertain the possibility that her feelings are related to the relationship's covert processes. For example, one trainee came to realise that her client was deliberately trying to get her angry so that he could then proclaim how unfairly he was being treated, thus protecting his fragile self-esteem but at the same time perpetuating his emotional disturbance. The trainee realised that this pattern was one often described by the client when the latter was talking about his social relationships in general. But in wrestling with her own 'I should not be feeling this way' feelings, the trainee was unable to gain insight into the client's pattern. In this case the group was successful in helping the trainee gain therapeutic understanding.

An Example of Case Discussion in the Seminar Group

In another seminar session Belinda, a trainee counsellor, was helped by the group to gain new insight into her relationship with Susan, her client. After describing the client's concerns and saying how the relationship had been progressing, Belinda asked how she could take the relationship 'deeper', since at times it seemed to her that they were simply having a cosy chat and that she was not helping Susan to explore the issues involved. Susan was a first-year university student and was struggling, so it seemed to Belinda, with ambivalent feelings about her dependence on her parents. She wanted to be independent of them but felt unable to tell them that she did not want them coming to visit her every weekend. Some members of the group suggested that Susan might also be angry with her parents but unable to express this for fear of hurting their feelings. Belinda recognised that one of the issues in her own life was her inability to show anger. When later on she said through gritted teeth that she had dealt with Susan's study problem (which had now re-emerged in their discussion), I suggested that she was feeling angry with her client, and pointed out my reasons for saying so. Belinda acknowledged that this might be the case but did not pursue the matter.

Belinda did, however, begin to talk about not wanting to be disliked by her client, at which point one member of the seminar group speculated that this might be related to her inability to take the relationship deeper. Belinda talked about needing to be a perfect counsellor and not daring to run the risk of being told by her client that she was inaccurate in her remarks (which is always a risk when attempting to take a therapeutic relationship 'deeper'). At this point, I asked Belinda how she had begun the last session, since it was in this session that they had become 'stuck' at a superficial level. Belinda remembered that in this session Susan had been strangely non-specific in her opening remarks, which had been punctuated with periods of silence. Belinda recalled how she had responded to this with anxiety, so she, 'for the client's benefit', had summarised what they had explored so far. This had led Susan to talk about her study problem again, which had made Belinda feel more comfortable but also aware that it was at times like these – i.e. times when she was very supportive to her client but this support seemed to be leading nowhere – that she experienced the 'cosy' superficiality of their relationship. A number of the trainees pointed out that Belinda's summarising statement had been for her own and not the client's benefit, and that by encouraging Susan to talk about a concrete problem, which suited Belinda's needs, she was encouraging a dependency relationship. This was a situation about which Belinda felt ambivalent: it led to the reduction of her own anxiety and meant she did not have to take risks and be wrong in helping Susan to explore her more central and deeper concerns, but it also prompted her to sense that they were not going beyond the superficial level in their relationship. This paralleled the ambivalence that Susan felt in her own life about being dependent on or independent from her parents and her boyfriend.

During the seminar, it was sometimes apparent that both the trainer and the trainees were going too fast for Belinda, and she was occasionally defensive in her statements. Both the timing of remarks made to the presenter and the pacing of the session are important variables to bear in mind, and although in this instance both were too quick for Belinda, she was able in her next individual supervision session to explore fruitfully the issues which the seminar group had brought to the surface.

Conclusion

As the preceding paragraph implies, case discussions are not always successful in achieving their aims. Sometimes in the seminar group, for example, the trainee's need to be defensive is such that the rest of the group loses patience with her and the trainee is not helped. The role of the trainer here is to comment on the covert processes of relationships between group members. At times too, the trainer may be able to use her own feelings to therapeutic effect, thus saving the situation. But, in situations where both the group members *and* the trainer are antagonistic to the case presenter, the seminar group may have an anti-therapeutic effect.

Case discussion as a training mode thus has its inherent difficulties. Used well, however, it can help trainees to learn, by experience, that what helps the client to develop is not the counsellor's technological skill but the quality of the counselling relationship. In this way, it can be of the utmost value in the training process.

References

BRUCH, M. (1974). *Learning Psychotherapy.* Cambridge, MA: Harvard University Press.
CARKHUFF, R.R. (1969). *Helping and Human Relations*, vol. 1. New York: Holt, Rinehart & Winston.
EGAN, G. (1975). *The Skilled Helper: A model for systematic helping and interpersonal relating*, 1st edn. Monterey, CA: Brooks/Cole.

EGAN, G. (1990). *The Skilled Helper: A systematic approach to effective helping*, 4th edn. Pacific Groves, CA: Brooks/Cole.

GENDLIN, E.T. (1964). A theory of personality change. In: P. Worchel and D. Bryne (Eds), *Personality Change.* New York: Wiley.

HAZELL, J. (1974). Counselling in higher education. *Education for Development*, 3(1), 3–14.

IVEY, A.E. (1971). *Microcounseling: Innovations in interviewing training.* Springfield, IL: Charles C. Thomas.

IVEY, A.E. (1988). *Intentional Interviewing and Counseling: Facilitating client development.* Pacific Groves, CA: Brooks/Cole.

PATTERSON, C.H. (1977). New approaches in counselling: healthy diversity or anti-therapeutic? *British Journal of Guidance and Counselling*, 5 (1), 19–25.

RIOCH, M.J., COULTER, W.R. and WEINBERGER, D.M. (1976). *Dialogues for Therapists.* San Francisco: Jossey-Bass.

ROGERS, C.R. and TRUAX, C.B. (1967). The therapeutic conditions antecedent to change: a theoretical view. In: C.R. Rogers, E.T. Gendlin, D.J. Kiesler and C.B. Truax (Eds), *The Therapeutic Relationship and Its Impact: A study of psychotherapy with schizophrenics.* Madison: University of Wisconsin Press.

Chapter 5
The Relevance of Research for Counsellors

Much counsellor training is devoted to skills development, personal development and the supervision of counselling practice. Few courses, however, other than those at Masters level, devote much time to exploring the relevance of research for practising counsellors. This has led to the situation in which counsellors devalue counselling research. Thus a survey published in 1978 showed that the membership of the British Association for Counselling (BAC) viewed research a low priority for BAC attention (Nelson-Jones and Coxhead, 1978). Whilst up-to-date data on this issue are not available, my impression is that this situation has not changed.

Thinking that part of the reason for counsellors' negative views about research could be traced to their doubts about the relevance of research studies for their work, I published this chapter in 1980 primarily for trainee counsellors. In doing so, I hoped to instil in them a positive view about the place of research in counselling at a formative stage of their development. Thus, I have used the chapter as a stimulus for discussion about counselling research ever since it was first published. I consider it to be a good example of the use of a published paper for training purposes.

Introduction

In this chapter current research paradigms are outlined and appraised to enable trainee counsellors to see more clearly the practical relevance of counselling research. The standpoint taken is that, although it is possible to criticise current research paradigms on a number of grounds, practitioners who know their own biases and the limitations of these paradigms can successfully experiment with interventions suggested by research in their own practice. An example is presented from the research on paralinguistic variables in client-centred counselling.

46

The Dominant Research Paradigm: Its Scope and Limitations

Current research in counselling is carried out either in actual clinical settings or, more often, in experimental laboratory settings. Whilst the latter inquiry is often called 'analogue' research, Kazdin (1978) has pointed out that all counselling research is analogous in so far as a situation is constructed which allows for the more-or-less controlled study of particular phenomena. Thus, even such a study as Sloane et al. (1975), which compared psychoanalytically oriented therapy and behaviour therapy by employing 'real' clients and experienced therapists, was an analogue of the clinical situation in that clients were told they were participating in a research study and were required to complete an extensive assessment battery on several occasions; this situation clearly differs from the normal clinical context where clients are *not* informed that they are participating in a research investigation and do *not* have to complete frequent assessment forms (Kazdin and Rogers, 1978).

Viewing all counselling research as analogous leads to the identification of dimensions along which a study can be evaluated in terms of the extent to which it is an analogue of the counsellor's normal working context. These dimensions include: client population, areas of client concern, treatment employed, client recruitment, and length of treatment. Kazdin (1978) has argued that 'the relation between an analogue study and generality to clinical situations for a given dimension itself is an area of research' (p.684). Such research is badly needed to enable counsellors to assess the degree of external validity of results gained from analogue studies (i.e. the extent to which results can be generalised to clinical situations). The existing evidence suggests that the relationship will be complex. Kushner (1978) found that the utility of an analogue as a predictor of real counselling behaviour depended on: (1) counsellor experience level; (2) how counsellor performance was measured; and (3) which dependent variables were employed in the analysis. If the complexity of Kushner's findings is widely replicated, then trainee counsellors can be excused if they throw their hands up in despair. I believe, however, that such a reaction would be precipitate and would – as will be suggested below – deprive trainee counsellors of a source of helpful guidelines for counselling practice.

The emphasis in the dominant research paradigm is on maximising internal validity, i.e. 'the extent to which a given set of procedures allows one to draw valid conclusions about what actually happened in an experiment' (Mahoney, 1978). The aim is to control as many factors as possible so that if an effect occurs it can be attributed to the independent variable(s). The issue of control is important here. Practitioners are often more concerned with *why* an effect occurs than *that* an effect occurs. Thus it is not enough for the trainee counsellor to know that, in a given experiment, systematic desensitisation helps students reduce their examination anxiety more than client-centred therapy. The question is 'why?'

To show that systematic desensitisation itself has greater therapeutic efficacy than a competing treatment, the researcher must show that the results cannot be attributed to such factors as: (1) differences in counsellors' expertise, experience and enthusiasm; (2) differences in clients' expectations and preferences regarding treatment; and (3) differences in perceived treatment credibility. In order to do this, the researcher must employ the relevant control groups. Even if these control groups are not employed, however, trainee counsellors can still employ systematic desensitisation in the treatment of examination anxiety in a spirit of open-minded inquiry, particularly if they pay attention to and deal therapeutically with clients' expectations, preferences and perceptions of treatment credibility. In addition, it is incumbent on the trainee counsellor to gain expertise and experience in the procedure and to carry it out with appropriate enthusiasm. If the trainee ignores clients' expectations, preferences and perceptions of treatment credibility, and carries out the procedure in an uninspired, inept fashion, it is unlikely that the procedure of systematic desensitisation will have enough specific therapeutic potency to negate these other negative factors (Kazdin and Wilcoxon, 1976). Thus, although trainnee counsellors should be sensitive to the quality of a given research study or group of studies, they can try out treatment interventions suggested as effective by poorly designed research studies.

Lazarus (1978) suggests that the dominant research paradigm has distinct limitations when it comes to tailoring systematic desensitisation for use with individual clients. He argues that research can help to determine *when* to use the procedure but not *how* to use it with a given client. He claims that its efficacy depends on 'the different ways in which I explain its rationale to specific clients, the individual pace, manner and structure I employ with different people, the variety of ways in which I introduce scenes, embroider images and embellish tailor-made themes. . .' (p.24). It remains to be seen to what extent studies carried out within the dominant research paradigm can answer the 'specificity' question: in which ways can different counsellors effectively employ systematic desensitisation with different clients? It is doubtful, however, whether Lazarus will get from such studies the information he requires to employ systematic desensitisation effectively with a given client.

One barrier to the application of findings derived from the dominant research paradigm stems from the fact that research reports in general do not indicate clearly enough *how* treatments are carried out. Thus, in a study comparing cognitive therapy and behaviour therapy in the treatment of depression, it is not sufficient for the researcher to provide independent evidence that treatment guidelines were followed (Shaw, 1977): he must also provide independent evidence with respect to how well the treatment was carried out. A somewhat different and interesting point of view has been expressed by Kazdin (1978) regarding treatment. He points out that if good results can be attributed to a treatment carried out by inexperienced counsellors in a standard fashion (which the dominant research paradigm requires), then greater confidence can be placed in the treatment's therapeutic potency than if the results were obtained by experienced therapists skilled in the treatment. He raises the possibility that the analogue situation may provide 'a more conservative test of a relation between treatment and therapeutic change than that provided in the clinical situation'.

It is hazardous, although not necessarily foolhardy, to make changes in one's counselling work on the basis of results from a single study. Garfield (1978) has argued that it is wise to view unreplicated findings as basically suggestive and to withhold final judgement until the findings have been replicated. Strict replications are, however, relatively rare in the counselling and psychotherapy research: a recent survey of contributors to the *Journal of Consulting and Clinical Psychology* revealed that replication of past research was viewed as a low priority (Kendall and Ford, 1979). Consequently, trainee counsellors should be tentative in putting into practice the findings from any one study. Results of the counsellor's attempts to put into practice the researcher's findings could, though, be fed back to the researcher, perhaps using a single-case experimental design (Hersen and Barlow, 1976), thus initiating a much-needed dialogue between researchers and practitioners.

A more reliable procedure would be for trainees to look at a group of studies on a relevant issue rather than extrapolating from isolated studies. But what if individual studies in a series or group of studies are seriously flawed? Are trainee counsellors justified in dismissing the area as having poor external validity because of poor internal validity? Strictly speaking yes, but practically they had better not. Orlinsky and Howard (1978) concur:

> If study after flawed study seemed to point significantly in the same direction we could not help believing that somewhere in all that variance there must be a reliable real effect (pp.288–289).

An example follows.

Implications of Research for Practice: An Example from Dominant Paradigm Research

A series of studies has been carried out within the client-centred framework on counsellor and client paralinguistic behaviour (Rice, 1965,

1973; Rice and Wagstaff, 1967; Duncan, Rice and Butler, 1968; Rice and Gaylin, 1973; Wexler, 1975; Wexler and Butler, 1976). The results of these studies indicate that (1) client expressiveness (expressive voice quality and connotative language) is significantly and positively related to counselling outcome and to level of client's psychological functioning; (2) in productive therapy sessions, counsellors focus on the client's inner experience, using fresh connotative language in an expressive fashion, speaking with normal stress, oversoft intensity and overlow pitch, and using open vocal fold control with unfilled pauses (i.e. they sound serious, warm, relaxed and concerned); and (3) a counsellor can improve the poor prognosis of an inexpressive client by stimulating the client's expressive participation with the counsellor's own expressive interventions.

These studies, however, had flaws which threaten both their internal and external validity. First, therapy outcome assessment was problematic. Change was not measured multidimensionally and also change criteria were not individualised. Changes in both behaviour and internal states were not assessed, and evaluation was too dependent on counsellor and client perspectives, i.e. changes were not assessed from the perspective of relevant others in the client's life or from the perspective of trained raters of outcomes. Secondly, the counsellors employed in the studies were not blind to the purposes of the studies. The series was originated and carried out at the University of Chicago Counseling Centre, and it may be that the counsellors there were particularly sensitive to the therapeutic potency of paralinguistic features and of expressiveness of communications since they would have been more aware of the research group's focus than most other client-centred practitioners. Thirdly, the studies were done within a client-centred framework 'in which the primary task of the therapist is to help the client to engage in a process of self-exploration with as much freshness and immediacy as possible' (Rice and Wagstaff, 1967). Thus the results may not be generalisable to other approaches which emphasise different counsellor primary tasks. In addition, the change process may not be the same for all counselling systems.

However flawed this set of studies may be, reliable effects were found which may well have implications for practising and trainee client-centred counsellors. They could well lead such counsellors to pay close attention to the paralinguistic style of their interventions and to experiment with making their interventions more expressive, particularly with inexpressive clients, while still remaining within the client's frame of reference. The effects of therapeutic procedures are, however, mediated by other factors as outlined earlier, e.g. client expectations. An important and often neglected mediating variable between a procedure and its effect is the counsellor-as-person.

One facet will be explored here. It may be that client-centred counsellors who deliberately try to make their interventions more expressive may be perceived as non-genuine in so doing. Schoeninger (1966) found that counsellors who were rated as genuine in their use of self-disclosure were more effective in making such interventions than counsellors rated as non-genuine in their use of self-disclosure. Thus there are hidden problems in applying even consistent research findings, since trainee counsellors who attempt to put into practice such findings vary across many dimensions, some of which may interact negatively with counsellor expressiveness. An additional problem with the research literature in this respect is that we know very little about the counsellors who carry out the treatments. More information is necessary here for trainee counsellors to make sense of the impact of counsellor-as-person variables on treatment efficacy.

As a result, 'cautious experimentation' with research findings is necessary, although this very attitude may affect the therapeutic value of interventions. This paradox should be accepted rather than lamented. One possible solution to the paradox would be for trainee counsellors to form 'research application' groups where the implications of research findings are discussed and new ways of intervening with clients tried out first in role-play and co-counselling situations.

Some Alternative Research Paradigms

The dominant paradigm in counselling research has recently been subjected to scrutiny from critics advocating alternative paradigms. Smail (1978), for example, has criticised counselling researchers for the over-emphasis they place on scientific control. The implicit assumption here is that subjects are static, and that this results in an alienating relationship between researchers and their subjects. Again, Goldman (1976) argues that counselling researchers should give up their scientific models which, whilst perhaps appropriate for use in the physical sciences, are not appropriate in the study of the counselling process. He argues for a contractual relationship between researcher and subjects where research-ers share with each subject, 'as much as possible, the goals of the study and what is going to happen, and seek an open and collaborative relationship with the subject before data are collected and before experimental interventions begin' (p.549).

One study where such a collaborative relationship between researcher and subjects was absent was carried out by Davies (1982) in which he assessed ten telephone counsellors' responses to him as he role-played a 'client' who was supposedly under pressure by his family to get married. What he did was to write down the responses of the counsellors as he enacted his role and then he analysed them according to a five-point scale of facilitative counsellor responding. He found that only three of the ten counsellors responded at a level which (according to his scale) could be considered facilitative. Whilst it is important to study the quality of help offered by counselling hotlines, it is my view that Davies's approach was questionable on ethical grounds.

First he deliberately deceived the counsellors into thinking that he was a 'real client'. He portrayed himself as a person in distress, when actually he was a person carrying out a research study pretending to be a person in distress. It is therefore possible to conclude that most counsellors in his study offered poor counselling to a researcher playing a role. However, given that most, if not all, of his 'subjects' were successfully deceived, and given that counselling research is a human transaction, to what extent should trainee counsellors regard the results of transactions where one participant showed bad faith as representative of transactions where both participants show good faith? It has been shown that members of the British Association for Counselling viewed research as a low priority for BAC attention (Nelson-Jones and Coxhead, 1978). My informal conversations with counsellors have shown me that they are concerned with the generalisability of research findings which are based on inauthentic encounters such as described by Davies.

Secondly, Davies did not obtain the informed consent of his 'subjects'. In most psychology experiments, subjects are at least invited to participate in a 'study'. They are then deceived as to the true purpose of the researcher but are 'de-briefed' after their participation has ended, i.e. the true purpose of the researcher is finally revealed. Davies neither invited counsellors to participate in his study nor debriefed them afterwards. Are counsellors less deserving of ethical treatment than clients in research studies?

However, it is important to study the quality of counselling offered by telephone hotlines. The question is, can we do so while gaining counsellors' informed consent, without employing deception *and* in a way in which the participating counsellors might benefit from the experience? I believe so. If I were conducting such a study, I would first contact the organisations concerned, openly disclose my purpose and invite participation from organisational representatives and volunteering counsellors. I would stress that we would need to collaborate on the enterprise and arrive at a methodology which would (1) help the organisation and participating counsellors to reflect non-defensively on any deficiencies in counselling skill that might be discovered, and (2) meet acceptable research criteria. Of course the results of such research might have less external validity than Davies's findings. However, they would be obtained from 'good faith' transactions and this may be more generalisable to other similar 'good faith' transactions than were Davies's results.

The paradigm which Goldman and Smail advocate and which I have alluded to in the example above can, of course, itself be criticised on a number of grounds. Internal validity might be threatened, since it may be difficult to attribute effects to a given source due to lack of control of interfering variables. The paradigm would be more concerned with identifying associations than causal relationships. But the point is that we will not find an infallible research paradigm: each one has its strengths and weaknesses. There is room for several paradigms, and if researchers discover similar findings from different paradigms, then they will be in a much stronger position to make practical recommendations to practising and trainee counsellors.

One variant of the 'contractual' research paradigm would be to focus on the unique features of an ongoing relationship and on the 'negotiated meanings' which emerge between the participants. As Smail (1978) has put it:

> What happens to one person in psychotherapy cannot be generalised (except with the greatest caution) to others because one person's psychotherapy involves a unique combination of two people's sets of meanings (his own and his therapist's).
>
> (p.57)

It is possible, however, that such unique relationships may share common features. The study of sets of meanings shared between counsellor and client and how these change over time is known as *process* research. The dominant research paradigm has so far failed to reveal much of value in its attempts to study process, since investigators have endeavoured to *impose* a meaningful structure on the raw data*. An alternative paradigm approach would involve *eliciting* meanings from the participants themselves. Kagan et al. (1967) have suggested that research- ers adopt an 'inquirer' role, in which they would help the counsellor and client reflect on the counselling process and would help them to identify, for example, episodes which were important in initiating change, i.e. critical incidents and the impact of these incidents on both participants from their own perspectives. It would be possible to chart the progress of counselling relationships in this way, so as to determine the unique and shared features of such relationships.

Another approach to the study of elicited meaning would be for both participants to keep diaries. Evans and Robinson (1978) report on the diary of a client who received 19 sessions of behaviour therapy. The authors concluded that 'the diary exposed us to the limitations of therapy and the crudity of our working model. . .'. Comparing clients' diaries and counsellors' accounts could yield interesting discrepancies from which counsellors could re-evaluate their work. The results of such studies could be then compared with process studies based on the dominant research paradigm with its emphasis on clarification by imposed meaning. Again there is room for both paradigms.

---

*This is truer now than it was when this chapter was witten.

The Bias of Research Consumers

It is possibly a truism to say that practising and trainee counsellors do not read research reports without bias. It is probable that their views of what is important in counselling affects their interpretation of research more often than research affects their view of what is important. Cohen and Suchy (1979) found that psychoanalytically oriented practitioners rated an outcome study as less methodologically adequate when the results of the study demonstrated the superiority of behaviour therapy than when the outcome favoured psychoanalytically oriented therapy. Although the study (which unbeknown to therapist raters was fictitious) involved short-term treatment (5 months) and was thus biased against psychoanalytically oriented therapy, therapists of that persuasion were not affected by this bias in general, but may have focused on it when the results did not support the efficacy of their therapeutic orientation. I, myself, have to monitor closely my adeptness at criticising studies that do not demonstrate the superiority of rational–emotive counselling (REC) whilst remaining relatively uncritical of research favouring my preferred approach. Mahoney (1977) and Meichenbaum (1977) have similarly criticised Ellis (1977) in this respect.

Thus it is important for trainee counsellors to be aware of their own biases and of how these might influence their reading of – and consequently their attempts at applying – research findings.

References

COHEN, L.H. and SUCHEY, K.R. (1979). The bias in psychotherapy research evaluation. *Journal of Clinical Psychology*, **35**, 184–187.

DAVIES, P.G.K. (1982). The functioning of British counselling hotlines: a pilot study. *British Journal of Guidance and Counselling*, **10**, 195–199.

DUNCAN, S. Jr, RICE, L.N. and BUTLER, J.M. (1968). Therapists' paralanguage in peak and poor psychotherapy hours. *Journal of Abnormal Psychology*, **73**, 556–570.

ELLIS, A. (1977). Rational–emotive therapy: research data that support the clinical and personality hypotheses of RET and other modes of cognitive–behaviour therapy. *The Counseling Psychologist*, **7**, 2–41.

EVANS, I.M. and ROBINSON, C.H. (1978). Behavior therapy observed: the diary of a client. *Cognitive Therapy and Research*, **2**, 335–355.

GARFIELD, S.L. (1978). Research on client values in psychotherapy. In: S.L. Garfield and A.E. Bergin (Eds), *Handbook of Psychotherapy and Behavior Change: An empirical approach*, 2nd edn. New York: Wiley.

GOLDMAN, L. (1976). A revolution in counseling research. *Journal of Counseling Psychology*, **23**, 543–552.

HERSEN, M. and BARLOW, D.H. (1976). *Single Case Experimental Designs*. New York: Pergamon.

KAGAN, N., KRATHWOHL, D.R., GOLDBERG, A.D., CAMPBELL, R.J., SHAUBLE, P.G., GREENBERG, B.S. et al. (1967). *Studies in Human Interaction: Interpersonal process recall simulated by videotape*. East Lansing: Educational Publication Services, Michigan State University.

KAZDIN, A.E. (1978). Evaluating the generality of findings in analogue therapy research. *Journal of Consulting and Clinical Psychology*, 46, 673–686.

KAZDIN, A.E. and ROGERS, T. (1978). On paradigms and recycled ideologies: analogue research revisited. *Cognitive Therapy and Research*, 2, 105–117.

KAZDIN, A.E. and WILCOXON, L.A. (1976). Systematic desensitization and nonspecific treatment effects: a methodological evaluation. *Psychological Bulletin*, 83, 729–758.

KENDALL, P.C. and FORD, J.D. (1979). Reasons for clinical characteristics of contributors and their contributions to the *Journal of Consulting and Clinical Psychology*. *Journal of Consulting and Clinical Psychology*, 47, 99–105.

KUSHNER K. (1978). On the external validity of two psychotherapy analogues. *Journal of Consulting and Clinical Psychology*, 46, 1394–1402.

LAZARUS, A.A. (1978). Science and beyond. *The Counseling Psychologist*, 7(3), 24–25.

MAHONEY, M.J. (1977). A critical analysis of rational–emotive theory and therapy. *The Counseling Psychologist*, 7, 44–46.

MAHONEY, M.J. (1978). Experimental methods and outcome evaluation. *Journal of Consulting and Clinical Psychology*, 46, 660–672.

MEICHENBAUM, D.H. (1977). Dr Ellis, please stand up. *The Counseling Psychologist*, 7, 43–44.

NELSON-JONES, R. and COXHEAD, P. (1978). Whither BAC: a survey of members' views on policy and priorities. *Counselling News*, No. 21, June, 2–5.

ORLINSKY, D.E. and HOWARD, K.I. (1978). The relation of process to outcome in psychotherapy. In: S.L. Garfield and A.E. Bergin (Eds), *Handbook of Psychotherapy and Behavior Change: An empirical approach*, 2nd edn. New York: Wiley.

RICE, L.N. (1965). Therapist's style of participation and case outcome. *Journal of Consulting Psychology*, 29, 155–160.

RICE, L.N. (1973). Client behavior as a function of therapist style and client resources. *Journal of Counseling Psychology*, 20, 306–311.

RICE, L.N. and GAYLIN, N.L. (1973). Personality processes reflected in client and vocal style and Rorschach processes. *Journal of Consulting and Clinical Psychology*, 40, 133–138.

RICE, L.N. and WAGSTAFF, A.K. (1967). Client voice quality and expressive style as indexes of productive psychotherapy. *Journal of Consulting Psychology*, 31, 557–563.

SCHOENINGER, D.W. (1966). Client experiencing as a function of therapist self-disclosure and pre-therapy training in experiencing. *Dissertation Abstracts International*, 26, 5551.

SHAW, B.F. (1977). Comparison of cognitive therapy and behavior therapy in the treatment of depression. *Journal of Consulting and Clinical Psychology*, 45, 543–551.

SLOANE, R.B., STAPLES, F.R., CRISTOL, A.H., YORKSTON, N.J. and WHIPPLE, K. (1975). *Psychotherapy Versus Behavior Therapy*. Cambridge, MA: Harvard University Press.

SMAIL, D.J. (1978). *Psychotherapy: A personal approach*. London: Dent.

WEXLER, D.A. (1975). A scale for the measurement of client and therapist expressiveness. *Journal of Clinical Psychology*, 31, 486–489.

WEXLER, D.A. and BUTLER, J.M. (1976). Therapist modification of client expressiveness in client-centred therapy. *Journal of Consulting and Clinical Psychology*, 44, 261–265.

Chapter 6
Using Rational–Emotive Counselling in the Supervision of Counsellors

As noted earlier I developed an interest in rational–emotive counselling (REC) in 1977. In this chapter (published in 1987) I show how REC methods can be used to help trainees overcome their anxieties about playing audio tapes of their counselling work in supervision. The first part of the chapter outlines ways in which such anxieties can become manifest in supervision, whilst the second part distinguishes between personal worth and 'fate control' anxieties and demonstrates how I have used REC in helping trainees address these issues.

Introduction

About a decade ago I discussed some of the advantages of employing audio-tape procedures in counselling and supervision (Dryden, 1981). I pointed out in that article that listening to trainee counsellors' accounts of their counselling sessions and hearing audio tapes of these sessions often reveals important discrepancies. For example, in a group supervision session, one trainee told the group about the interventions she employed with a client experiencing extreme examination anxiety. She stated that she covered a number of important concepts with the client. She discussed with him: (1) the important healing qualities of unconditional self-acceptance; (2) the mediating effects that cognitions have on emotional experience; (3) the value of focusing on task-relevant cognitions and editing out task-irrelevant thoughts in evaluative situations; (4) the benefit of concentrating on one piece of revision at a time rather than on the entire revision schedule; and (5) the importance of taking regular short breaks from study. She indicated that the client understood these concepts and received great benefit from the discussion. However, while listening to the tape of the session, it emerged that the trainee covered all of these points in one long 90-second statement. Whilst the client claimed to understand these concepts, it was obvious to all that he was confused. The value of recording counselling sessions is therefore apparent.

However, trainees often experience anxiety about using cassette recorders in counselling and supervision and this theme will be developed in the present chapter.

Manifestations of Trainee Recording and Supervision Anxiety

Supervision of trainees' audio-taped counselling sessions was an important component of the 1-year postgraduate Diploma in Counselling in Educational Settings' course offered at Aston University (1970–1984). Prospective trainees were informed of this and they knew that places on the course were contingent upon their agreement to make tapes of actual counselling sessions. In the first term of the course, trainees taped their peer-counselling sessions and thus became quite familiar with being recorded while counselling. They should have thus achieved a fair measure of habituation to making audio tapes of counselling sessions before seeing clients on placement. However, a significant number of trainees initially experienced debilitating anxiety which interfered both with their counselling work and with their ability to learn from supervision. This anxiety generally took several different forms.

Showing over-concern for clients

A number of trainees expressed exaggerated concern for the impact that recording counselling sessions had on clients. They feared that clients would be psychologically damaged if they even raised the topic of tape recording. In my many years' experience of asking clients for permission to record sessions, the vast majority readily agree and, as far as I am aware, none were damaged by my request. My practice is to be thoroughly honest in my request. I point out that it is helpful for me to listen back to sessions and to receive supervision on them. I guarantee that only my supervisor and supervision group will listen to them and that the tapes will be wiped clean afterwards. I tell clients that whilst taping sessions is helpful to me, my primary concern is for their well-being. If they prefer not to have sessions recorded, their wish will be respected and I emphasise the primacy of their decision. When I discussed this with trainees, they were often then able to express their own anxiety underlying their stated concern for clients – anxiety concerning the impact that recording counselling sessions would have on *them*.

'I don't have a tape this week'

In my experience of supervising tapes, I have been impressed with the range of 'reasons' which trainees give either for not making tapes or for not having audible tapes of counselling sessions for supervision. This occurs despite the fact that they receive clear instructions concerning the attainment of clearly audible tape recordings. The 'reasons' I have received can be grouped as follows:

Plug faults

● The plug did not contain a fuse
● The plug contained a defective or incorrect fuse
● The plug wires were not properly attached.

Mains faults

● The mains lead was not attached to the recorder
● The mains lead was not inserted into the wall socket
● The socket switch was not turned on.

Microphone faults

● The external microphone was not attached (or not properly attached) to the recorder
● Batteries were not inserted into the battery-operated microphone
● The microphone was placed incorrectly so that clear recording could not be obtained
● The external microphone was not powerful enough to register voices clearly.

Battery faults

● Batteries were not inserted into the battery-operated recorder
● 'Dead' or fading batteries were used (batteries not regularly checked)
● Batteries were incorrectly inserted into the recorder
● Too few batteries were inserted into the recorder
● Batteries were left in the recorder causing corrosion
● The battery pack had not been recharged
● The battery pack had been incorrectly inserted into the recorder.

Recording faults

● Incorrect controls were depressed while 'recording'
● No controls were depressed while 'recording'
● A radio programme was recorded instead of the counselling session (when a radio-cassette recorder was used)
● An indistinct recording was made (either because an internal microphone was employed which was not sensitive enough to record clearly or because recording and erasing heads were not regularly cleaned).

Recorder faults

● The recorder was faulty in 'recording' mode
● Interference was present on the recording
● The recorder picked up local police or taxi broadcasts in 'recording' mode which masked the recording of the counselling session.

Tape faults

● No tape was inserted into the recorder
● The tape was incorrectly inserted into the recorder
● The tape was inappropriate for recording purposes.

Trainees who were not particularly anxious about recording counselling sessions generally made clearly audible cassette recordings which they regularly brought to supervision. Thus, it is probable that anxious trainees *tacitly* (i.e. outside their awareness) developed self-defeating ways of defending against their own anxiety. Helping these trainees to acknowledge their anxiety proved difficult, but was best done by encouraging them to explore how they would feel if they had made audible tapes which they would then present for supervision.

Trainee behaviour in counselling sessions

The behaviour that anxious trainees manifested in counselling sessions often provided clues to their recording and supervision anxiety. Such trainees were often 'forgetful'; they 'forgot' to take their recorder (microphone, cassettes or mains lead) to the sessions or they 'forgot' to introduce the topic of recording at the beginning of counselling interviews. When they did remember, they claimed that their clients were 'far too upset' to make clear decisions concerning recording. When they did introduce the topic to clients, they did so hesitantly or ineptly so that their clients refused.

When they did record their sessions they tended to: (1) play safe, by being extremely passive in interviews or by parroting client statements verbatim; (2) talk too much and ask irrelevant questions when silences occurred; (3) display many paraverbal clues to anxiety; and (4) often misunderstand what their clients were trying to express.

Trainee behaviour in supervision

Trainees who were particularly anxious about recording their counselling sessions often displayed typical behaviour patterns in supervision. They often: (1) 'forgot' to bring in tapes for supervision; (2) brought in the 'wrong' tape; (3) tried to engage the supervisor and/or the supervision group in theoretical discussions about the counselling process; (4) opted to present their tapes last hoping for a truncated period of supervision; (5) spent considerable periods of supervision time trying to find the precise segment of tape which they wished to play; (6) tended to deny or distort positive feed-back; (7) played segments of counselling sessions which contained plenty of client talk but little counsellor intervention; and (8) played numerous 'games' that have been admirably documented by Kadushin (1968) which were designed to distract supervisors' attention from their actual counselling work.

Understanding Trainee Recording and Supervision Anxiety

It was important in attempting to understand trainees' anxiety about recording counselling sessions to focus on the inferences that they made and the beliefs they held about the recording and supervision process.

Inferential distortions

Inferences are cognitive processes that are either interpretative and/or evaluative in nature, but do not themselves account for people's emotional experiences. They indicate how people interpret the data that are available to them in their perceptual field. Inferences can of course be accurate or distorted. They are best regarded as hypotheses about the nature of reality and can thus be subjected to empirical inquiry. Unfortunately, anxious trainees often regarded their inferences as facts and thus not amenable to such inquiry. Since anxiety is an emotion that generally involves anticipations of future threat, it is not surprising to find that anxious trainees frequently made a number of distorted inferences concerning the future implications of their present behaviour. Identifying such inferential distortions was done by either examining trainees' in vivo automatic thoughts (Beck et al., 1979) or by helping them to articulate the private meanings that the recording and supervision process held for them. Burns (1980) has developed the pioneering work of Aaron Beck (compare Beck et al., 1979) on the common forms of inferential distortions that depressed and anxious clients typically make. Burns's 'ten forms of twisted thinking' will be used as a framework for presenting the most common inferential errors that anxious trainees make concerning the personal implications of the recording and supervision process.

All-or-nothing thinking

Here trainees typically employed black-or-white categories to process information. All-or-nothing thinking commonly leads to perfectionism and feelings of failure. Thus, one trainee reported observing herself making an inaccurate summary of her client's concerns and concluded: 'I've ruined this interview completely.'

Over-generalisation

Anxious trainees often saw a single event as a perpetual pattern of defeat. Words like 'always' and 'never' are clues that over-generalisations were being made. Such trainees often become easily discouraged and hopeless about their ability to learn and internalise constructive counselling skills. One trainee reported thinking that if he did not master the technique of systematic desensitisation quickly, then he would never learn it.

Mental filter

Commonly, anxious trainees focused on a single negative detail and dwelt on it obsessively so that their ability to make objective perceptions of reality became impaired. One trainee became so anxious about gaining her clients' approval that she habitually gave them extra time instead of terminating sessions punctually. She reported having the thought that, if one of her clients showed disapproval, then she would continually focus on this, thus editing out the total picture which indicated that many of her clients were benefiting quite well from their counselling sessions with her.

Disqualifying the positive

Anxious trainees tended to reject positive experiences when they occurred by saying that they didn't count. Such processes frequently occurred in supervision groups. For example, one trainee consistently denied that he was doing well with a socially anxious client (he was in fact helping her quite considerably), insisting that it was such an easy case (which it wasn't) that anybody would have been successful.

Jumping to conclusions

Anxious trainees often acted as if they had extrasensory perception. They consistently interpreted events in a negative manner in the absence of corroborating evidence. There are two major types of 'conclusion-jumping': mind-reading and negative prediction.

Mind-reading

Here anxious trainees predicted that their clients would have negative thoughts about them, the counselling process and the issue of tape recording. They regarded such inferences as 'facts' as opposed to 'hypotheses' and thus rarely attempted to test their validity. For example, one trainee came to supervision in a distressed state because she was certain that one of her clients had not kept an appointment because he regarded her as a 'useless novice'. It transpired that the client had been involved in a minor traffic accident, had tried to contact the counselling service by telephone to cancel his appointment but could not get through. In counselling, practitioners are not commonly in a position to ascertain reasons for client non-attendance and drop-out. Consequently, such ambiguity contributes to the perpetuation of self-defeating mind-reading.

Negative prediction
Anxious trainees often anticipated that counselling sessions would turn out badly and thus they frequently predicted disasters. One trainee predicted that he would fail to understand his new overseas client, and got into an anxious state which severely interfered with his ability to listen and emphasise with the client. As can be seen, negative predictions often become self-fulfilling prophecies.

Magnification and/or minimisation

In magnification, anxious trainees exaggerated the importance of their difficulties in learning and internalising counselling skills. They 'forgot' that most people would be uncomfortable learning new techniques and methods and regarded their discomfort in a very negative light. In minimisation, trainees undervalued their own skills and talents while praising their fellow trainees for these very same skills and talents.

Emotional reasoning

This occurs when people assume that their feelings constitute evidence as to the nature of reality. Thus, anxious trainees concluded that their anxiety was valid proof for their inadequacy as counsellors. One trainee argued that taping counselling sessions was dangerous because he felt anxious about it.

Labelling

This is an extreme form of overgeneralisation. Instead of acknowledging that they merely made errors or poorly executed counselling interventions, anxious trainees were much more likely to conclude that they were 'inadequate counsellors' than did less anxious trainees. The latter were more likely to acknowledge their errors in skill and technique without placing a pejorative label on their ability as counsellors.

Personalisation

Here anxious trainees were prone to assume almost total responsibility for the counselling process when it was going badly and virtually no responsibility when it was going well. They tended to be constantly looking for evidence that their clients were dissatisfied with their services. This vigilance perpetuated their anxiety which consequently impeded their learning. Trainees who were to be seen frequently checking for the arrival of unpunctual clients often made such personalising inferences.

Personal worth and fate control

The analysis presented above provides a helpful way of classifying the inferential distortions made by trainees anxious about recording and presenting their counselling interviews for supervision. Most frequently, trainees' inferential distortions reflect concerns about either *personal worth* or *fate control*. It is important to note that the same inferential distortions may therefore reflect these very different underlying concerns. For example, consider Jack and Sylvia, two counselling trainees who were both anxious in case what they considered to be poor examples of counselling technique would incur the disapproval of their respective supervisors. Both predicted that such disapproval was virtually certain to occur. However, while Jack was anxious because he was basing his personal worth on his supervisor's anticipated response, Sylvia was anxious that her supervisor's disapproval would influence him to give her poor job references which would, in her mind, ruin her career in counselling before it had commenced. Sylvia thus viewed her supervisor as having enormous control over her fate, whilst Jack viewed his supervisor as having enormous control over his personal worth.

Trainees who experienced 'personal worth' anxiety tended to predict that their errors (which they inevitably made in learning how to counsel) would lead their supervisors and fellow trainees to make negative judgements, not only of their counselling ability but also of their personal worth. They thus implicitly construed other people as harsh critics, intolerant of human fallibility. This (as will be shown later) was really a projection of their own intolerant attitude towards themselves. They were really harsh critics of themselves. However, trainees with 'fate control' anxiety predicted that their supervisors would note their errors and use this information against them in ways that would adversely affect their future aspirations (e.g. by giving them failing grades or writing them poor references etc.). They did not consider that their supervisors viewed such errors as an inevitable part of learning new skills. They thus construed their supervisors as malevolent individuals who would not make allowances for the fundamental processes of human learning. Again, as will be shown later, this view was generally a projection of their own attitude towards themselves and the world. They believed that they must not make errors and, when they did, they would consequently be punished. They sometimes did fail to gain their counselling qualification, but this was to a large extent a self-fulfilling prophecy because their 'fate control' anxiety seriously impaired their ability to learn from the feed-back that they were given.

Irrational beliefs

It is a fundamental assumption of REC that inferential distortions stem from people's irrational beliefs (Ellis, A., personal communication). Irrational beliefs are evaluations of personal significance couched in devout, dogmatic and absolute terms. They reflect a philosophy of demandingness and are stated as 'musts', 'shoulds', 'oughts' and 'have-to's' and generally account for people's emotional experiences.

Dryden (1984) has argued that there are two fundamental human disturbances – *ego disturbance* and *discomfort disturbance* – which of course take a myriad of different forms. Trainees who experienced 'personal worth' anxiety were clearly exemplifying ego disturbance. They profoundly believed the idea: 'that you can give yourself a global rating as a human and that your general worth and self-acceptance depends on the goodness of your performances and the degree that people approve of you' (Ellis, 1977a). They tended to make global ratings of their 'selves' which were conditional on (1) their counselling abilities, (2) the extent to which their clients improved and (3) the feed-back they received from their supervisors and, to a lesser extent, their fellow trainees. They overgeneralised from rating their present performance as trainee counsellors to rating their full potential ability as counsellors and thence made global ratings of their 'selves'. If they could articulate their underlying philosophy it would be thus: 'Because I am not doing very well at the moment in my counselling, I will never do well and therefore will always be an ineffective counsellor which will prove that I am worthless.' The statement: 'I am worthless' is derived from the premise: 'I must do well and be approved'. Believing this, they remained anxious even when they performed well, because they further believed that they *must* maintain that good performance in the future. These irrational beliefs underpin the inferential distortions that this group of anxious trainees made concerning the reactions of their clients, supervisors and fellow trainees. Since they were harsh critics of themselves, they once again predicted that others would make similarly harsh judgements of them.

Trainees who had discomfort disturbance wanted to enter the counselling profession, but escalated their desires into absolute demands. Their underlying philosophy was 'I must get what I want at all costs'. If they did not get what they believe they must, they concluded that *it was awful* and that they *could not stand* being deprived. Since they regarded getting what they wanted as absolutely necessary, they tended to be extremely sensitive to perceived threats to goal attainment. This underlying belief then accounted for their inferential distortions, since even constructive negative feed-back constituted a severe threat to what they believed they must have. Other people, and as has been noted particularly their supervisors, were thus seen as malevolent individuals who would deprive them of their sacred goals and, consequently, were viewed as having enormous control over their fate. These trainees did not necessarily attach their personal worth to the attainment of their goals, although some may have also done this. Trainees with 'pure' discomfort disturbance believed that they must get what they wanted merely because they desired it, whilst other trainees with ego disturbance believed that they must get what they wanted in order to prove to themselves that they were worthwhile individuals.

As Dryden, Trower and Casey (1983) have shown, ego disturbance and discomfort disturbance are often interacting processes. Thus, one trainee who believed that she must do well in counselling interviews (ego disturbance) became anxious. This anxiety activated her belief that she could not stand feeling anxious (discomfort disturbance), which in turn triggered her further belief that such heightened anxiety proved her worthlessness (ego disturbance). Indeed many trainees trapped themselves in the interlocking web of their ego and discomfort-related beliefs.

In the previous section, trainee anxiety about the recording and supervision process was considered. The manifestations of this anxiety were detailed and a framework for understanding its determinants was outlined. The emphasis of this section will be on how supervisors can help trainees overcome the debilitating effects of recording and supervision anxiety so that they can maximise their learning.

Overcoming Obstacles to Trainee Learning: Fostering a Helpful Climate in Supervision

It is important to realise that whilst not all trainees will be anxious about presenting audio tapes of their counselling sessions for supervision, virtually all will be apprehensive. As a supervisor I have found that applying the following principles is most beneficial in fostering a helpful climate in both individual and group supervision sessions. The promotion of a helpful climate is highly desirable if anxious trainees are to be encouraged to acknowledge and deal with their anxieties.

Unconditional acceptance

It is beneficial if supervisors show that they can unconditionally accept their trainees as fallible human beings. This means that whilst supervisors may rate certain aspects, behaviours or skills which their trainees may display, they endeavour not to rate the 'personhood' of trainees (Ellis,

1972). For example, I once had occasion to reproach one of my trainees thus for consistent unpunctuality at counselling sessions.

> Look, frankly I consider your behaviour in this regard to be pretty bad. We've discovered some of the reasons for it and though you claim to understand why you do it, you keep doing it. However, I want you to know that while I dislike your behaviour, I really don't feel badly at all about you as a total complex ever-changing person. While I think your behaviour stinks, you're not a stinker. And of course we've discovered that you have a lot of assets in your counselling. Now the reality is that counsellors who aren't punctual...

The trainee in question appreciated the honest expression of my annoyance concerning her behaviour and realised that I was not either in tone or words damning her as a person.

Supervisors would be wise to dispute their own internal intolerant demands about the behaviour of their trainees and replace these with their honest undevout preferences. In this way they will be able effectively to communicate unconditional acceptance of trainees, whilst honestly expressing their positive and negative reactions to trainee behaviour, when appropriate.

Supervisor self-disclosure

Anxious trainees often view their supervisors as infallible and fantasise that such superhuman beings learned how to counsel effortlessly and without error. It is important for supervisors to refuse to be seduced into this fantasy and openly acknowledge their past and present counselling errors. This serves to help trainees learn that: (1) errors are an inevitable part of becoming skilled counsellors; (2) counsellors do not suddenly stop making errors after completion of training; (3) it is possible to acknowledge errors openly without defensiveness and self-blame; and (4) supervisors who are tolerant of their own errors are likely to be tolerant of trainees' errors.

Explaining the nature of human learning

It is often helpful if supervisors discuss the nature of human learning with trainees at an early stage in the supervision process. It is important to stress that making errors is a natural and inevitable stage of learning any new set of complex skills – including counselling. In fact, I have found it useful to introduce a note of levity into this discussion. I usually add that any trainee who does not make errors will be ceremoniously thrown out of the supervision group. I also challenge and overthrow the myth that trainee counsellors will seriously damage clients by their errors – adding of course that this group will be the exception and I shall thus order several ambulances to stand by to ferry quivering clients to the nearest sanctuary called 'The Dryden home for clients damaged by trainees'. I, of course, stress that there is usually a long waiting list!

Employing the judicious use of humour

As can be seen from the above, I sometimes judiciously use humour in running supervision groups in a similar manner to its use in counselling. I do so because basically I agree with Ellis (1977b) who argues that one way of viewing emotional disturbance is that it stems from people taking themselves, others and the world *too* seriously. Anxious trainees definitely take themselves, the counselling role and the counselling process *too* seriously. I have found it highly therapeutic to challenge this viewpoint directly and indirectly with humour. I am often the butt of my own jokes (it is helpful to introduce humour into supervision in this way) and show in this manner that I do not take myself *too* seriously both in and out of counselling sessions. I show that I can laugh at some of the stupid things I have done while taking a compassionate and accepting attitude towards myself. The therapeutic use of humour with trainees had better be done within a spirit of unconditional acceptance. My intention is to direct my humorous comments to what trainees *do* and never at who they *are*. It is important for supervisors to elicit feed-back from trainees concerning the impact of humorous interventions. Not all trainees appreciate it and find it helpful!

Giving balanced feed-back

I have found that trainees benefit most from receiving *both* positive *and* constructive negative feed-back from their supervisors concerning their counselling work. Supervisors who consistently focus on trainees' errors unwittingly reinforce the self-defeating attitudes of trainees with 'personal worth' and 'fate control' anxieties. The receipt of consistent negative feed-back encourages trainees with 'personal worth' anxiety to blame themselves for their errors and those with 'fate control' anxiety to think that their future aspirations are being seriously threatened, since the supervisor concerned will surely give them failing grades. However, receiving consistent positive feed-back does not encourage either group of trainees to believe that they are learning very much about counselling. Whilst such feed-back may not directly evoke their respective anxieties, it does lead to a different kind of anxiety. Such trainees are reasonably sure that they are making counselling errors but are never told what they are. They either become anxious about this uncertainty or anxious about their own inability to determine their errors for themselves.

I thus strive to provide a balance between positive and constructive negative feed-back given in a spirit of unconditional acceptance of trainees as people. I even reinforce this with humour by saying to trainees with 'personal worth' anxiety: (1) 'that was a good response, but it doesn't make you a great person' and (2) 'that wasn't a very good response, but it doesn't make you a rotten person'. To trainees with 'fate control' anxiety I may say: (1) 'that wasn't a particularly good response, but we won't throw you out just yet', and (2) 'that was a good response, we'll definitely throw you out if you keep that standard up'.

Parenthetically, when giving trainees either positive or constructive negative feed-back, it is best to make such feed-back as *concrete* as possible. Vague feed-back does not encourage trainees to identify what they are doing right or wrong, and in the latter case they are not helped to consider specific alternatives.

Explaining 'personal worth' and 'fate control' anxieties

It is beneficial to explain to trainees at an early stage the nature of 'personal worth' and 'fate control' anxieties and to point out that these are both common, albeit dysfunctional, experiences. Providing such explanations makes it easier for trainees honestly to admit to these fears and it thus undercuts trainee defensiveness. This is particularly so when trainees can see that others in the group share similar anxieties. It is this factor of 'universality' that helps the supervision group become a therapeutic milieu for its members (Yalom, 1975). When trainees see that they are not alone in experiencing anxiety about the recording and supervision process, they tend to feel less shameful of these fears and thus become less defensive about their experiences.

Overcoming Obstacles to Trainee Learning: Dealing with Trainee Anxiety in Supervision

Whilst it is important to delineate boundaries between supervision and personal therapy, I find that the two processes sometimes necessarily overlap. When the factors described in the previous section do not help to allay fully trainees' fears, it is beneficial if supervisors help trainees to identify and deal with their anxieties if the latter are to maximise their learning from the supervisory experience. However, these therapeutic encounters are generally restricted to an exploration of trainees' anxieties about recording and supervision, and supervisors had better not deal with trainees' other personal problems in the supervision group since this tends to lead to difficult role-conflict problems. When I attempt to deal with trainees' recording- and supervision-related anxieties in supervision groups, I find it best to first seek permission to do this. I explain to the trainee in question that we could deal with the issue here in the group setting or, if the trainee prefers, the issue could be dealt with outside in personal therapy with someone else. If permission is not sought and granted, trainees may become understandably defensive during the ensuing discussion. Once permission is granted, my role is then to help trainees identify, challenge and change the inferential distortions and the irrational beliefs that underline their anxieties and negative inferences.

The following segments, then, represent two examples of how to deal with trainees' anxieties about recording and supervision in the context of supervision groups.

Dealing with 'personal worth' anxiety

Stephanie, the trainee in question, had on several occasions failed to bring audio tapes of her counselling sessions to the group for supervision.

Supervisor:	OK Stephanie, I would like to say something here. My guess is that you may have some anxiety about making tapes or presenting them for supervision here and this issue needs addressing in some context. What do you think?
Trainee:	Well.... I guess you are right... I know I don't like making tapes. It does seem to be valuable ... for other people. I guess I'm anxious about it. It certainly is on my mind a lot.
Supervisor:	OK, look. We can either discuss it here and now or if you wish you can discuss it with someone else... I mean ... with someone else not concerned with your evaluation. [The supervisor gives the trainee a *choice* to deal with the issue in the group or elsewhere. He seeks *permission* to discuss it further.]
Trainee:	Well... since we're here, why don't we do it now.
Supervisor:	All right. Now would you agree with my hunch that you're anxious?
Trainee:	Yes, that's right.
Supervisor:	What are you anxious about specifically?
Trainee:	Well ... if I knew no-one would listen to my tapes, I wouldn't mind recording my interviews. It's just ... the thought of ... well ... you all hearing my counselling.
Supervisor:	So you're anxious about the group listening to you on tape. What's scary about that?
Trainee:	Oh God! ... well ... it's the ... thought I guess about what you all ... no perhaps more about what you specifically are going to think of me.
Supervisor:	Right. You're scared that I'm going to think you're a great woman and a scholar. Is that correct? [General laughter. The supervisor uses humour to loosen the trainee up a little.]
Trainee: (laughs)	Well hardly. I guess I'm scared ... that ... you would think badly of me if I presented a lousy tape.
Supervisor:	But let's assume that. Let's suppose you played a lousy tape, what sort of things do you think I would think of you? [The supervisor checks out the nature of the trainee's inferences.]
Trainee:	Well ... (pause) ... the thing that comes to mind is that ... well the word idiot comes to mind.
Supervisor:	So you're scared that you'd present a tape and I'd think what an idiot you were for doing a lousy job? Is that it?
Trainee:	Yes.
Supervisor:	Now let's assume that I actually do think you're an idiot. Do you also get

	the sense that I would act on that thought in some way? [The supervisor seeks to go deeper into the trainee's inference structure. He wishes to assess what type of anxiety – 'personal worth' or 'fate control' – he is dealing with.]
Trainee:	I'm not sure ... what do you mean?
Supervisor:	Well, for example, do you think that I might shout at you and say something like: 'Stephanie you're an idiot', or do you think I'd fail you, or...?
Trainee:	Oh, I see ... No, I don't think you would shout at me. I don't think you'd fail me either. It's just ... I guess that your opinion is pretty important to me. [The trainee provides clues that it is 'personal worth' rather than 'fate control' anxiety that she is experiencing.']
Supervisor:	Pretty important in what sense?
Trainee:	Mmm... That I need you to think well of me.
Supervisor:	And if I don't?
Trainee:	Then I'd feel pretty lousy.
Supervisor:	Could you zero in on that feeling a little more and let me know what kind of lousy feeling it would be?
Trainee:	I'd feel depressed.
Supervisor:	What would you dwell on in that depressed lousy feeling?
Trainee:	On ... what a failure I am.
Supervisor:	So if I understand you. You would play a lousy tape. I would think you were an idiot, you would define yourself as a failure and feel lousy. Is that how it would go?
Trainee:	Yes, that's it.
Supervisor:	OK. Now as I see it, whether I think you are an idiot is important but not the real issue. You probably need to check it out, however, at some point. Can you see though the link between that definition 'I am a failure' and that lousy depressed feeling? [The supervisor focuses the trainee on her irrational belief, while indicating also the importance of testing inferences.]
Trainee:	Yes I see it. I'ts what you said in your lecture on REC, isn't it?
Supervisor:	Right. Now what I also said in that lecture is the importance of checking out whether that belief holds water. As Ellis might say, we want evidence that you would be a failure if you fail to impress me or fail to give a good performance.
Trainee:	Well there isn't any. I guess I'd be what you called a fallible human being who is failing to do well at the moment.
Supervisor:	That's correct, but look at how hesitantly you said that. You acknowledge it but don't really believe it.
Trainee:	Exactly.
Supervisor:	How do you think you could really work on believing it?
Trainee:	By going over it as you said in the lecture.
Supervisor:	Right. Really show yourself that (1) you don't need my approval and (2) if you were a failure you would do what?
Trainee:	Fail continually.
Supervisor:	At everything? Now if you really worked on that, would you feel anxious about my defining you in my own head as an idiot?
Trainee:	No, but I still wouldn't like it.
Supervisor:	Quite.

Trainee: But I wouldn't be anxious.
Supervisor: OK. Now if you really believed that, would you then be so sure of what
                I would be thinking of you?
Trainee: Let me see ... No ... I would still have doubts though.
Supervisor: Right. How could you check out your hunch about what I was thinking?
Trainee: By asking you?
Supervisor: No, by consulting the tea leaves. [General laughter.]
Trainee: OK! OK! I get your point.
(laughs)
Supervisor: Why don't you do that work and let us know how you get on next week.
                OK?
Trainee: OK.

Stephanie really worked on her 'personal worth' anxiety, started to accept herself unconditionally and began to bring in tapes regularly for supervision and did very well in her final assessment.

Dealing with 'fate control' anxiety

Ralph, another trainee, did bring in his audio tapes for supervision, but wasted an inordinate amount of time by discussing theoretical points, by trying to find the exact segment of tape he wished the group to hear and by extending other trainees' supervision time, so that his counselling work wasn't heard.

Supervisor: Well, Ralph. You seem to be doing it again. We're interested in hearing
                your counselling, not your excellent grasp of theory. Listen. Let me
                honestly ask you. Why are you so reluctant to play your tapes in here?
                You say you're not, but your behaviour belies your words.
Trainee: I'm not reluctant.
Supervisor: Let me put it another way. Close your eyes a moment. Really picture this
                scene. We are going to devote the whole 3-hour session to listening to
                your tapes and we won't allow you to interrupt or anything ... Now really
                picture that scene. How do you honestly feel? [The supervisor uses the
                imagery modality to bypass the trainee's tendency to deny feelings
                (Lazarus, 1984).]
Trainee: Quite uncomfortable.
Supervisor: OK. Now I'd like to explore that feeling more so that I can help you
                participate more in the group and play your tapes, but I don't want to
                force you. Would you like to explore this discomfort here and now? [The
                supervisor asks for permission to explore the issue further.]
Trainee: OK. [The trainee is hesitant, but the supervisor decides to go along with
                his stated agreement.]
Supervisor: Now what would you be uncomfortable about?
Trainee: About you lot listening to my tapes.
Supervisor: If you really focus on that discomfort, what kind of feeling would it be?
Trainee: ... A mixture of anger and anxiety.
Supervisor: Anxiety about what?
Trainee: Being evaluated.

Supervisor: By whom?

Trainee: Mmmh... mainly you. Yes by you.

Supervisor: And the anger?

Trainee: Towards you for making me do it.

Supervisor: OK. Let's go back to your anxiety. What kind of evaluation would you be afraid of getting?

Trainee: A bad one.

Supervisor: OK. Now let's assume, and I want to stress that we're assuming now, let's assume that I do listen to your tapes and give you a bad evaluation. What would be scary about that?

Trainee: I'd be scared that I wouldn't get my counselling diploma.

Supervisor: Let's assume that for the moment. If you don't get your diploma what would that mean? [The supervisor is aiming to 'chain' the trainee's inferences to get at his core irrational belief.]

Trainee: That would be awful.

Supervisor: Why is that?

Trainee: Counselling is really what I want to do. I've set my heart on it.

Supervisor: But let's say you were barred forever from your first choice, what then?

Trainee: ... well ... I don't know ... I'd hate it. It's just a feeling that ... I just have to get ... my first choice. [The trainee reveals in halting fashion his discomfort disturbance.]

Supervisor: OK. So you start by saying that counselling is really important to you and then you jump, if I understand you correctly, to you *have to* do it. Am I hearing you accurately?

Trainee: Yes.

Supervisor: So your belief is: 'Because it's important to me, I have to get it' or to put it another way, 'I have to get what I want'.

Trainee: That's right.

Supervisor: And then I guess, in your mind, I'm the obstacle.

Trainee: Right. It's funny, that's why I get angry with you. I often see you as kind of in control of ... my future almost. [The trainee clearly reveals his 'fate control' anxiety.]

Supervisor: Is there any feeling at all, that if you don't get to be a counsellor that you'd be less worthy or anything like that. [The supervisor is testing to see whether 'personal worth' anxiety is involved in the trainee's concerns.]

Trainee: No. It's much more the feeling of being deprived of what I want. I'd really hate that.

The supervisor then helped Ralph over subsequent weeks to acknowledge his desire to enter the counselling profession, but to dispute the belief that he *had to* get what he wanted. Ralph was further helped to imagine his future without counselling and eventually began to see that he could be happy in his second or third career choice, although not as happy as he would be working as a counsellor. This helped him to view his supervisor as less of a threat, although some direct interventions were still necessary to help him correct some of his inferential 'fate control' distortions. He passed the course with average grades.

Whilst I have chosen to present examples where trainees revealed 'personal worth' and 'fate control' anxieties in their pure form, in reality much trainee anxiety is a subtle blend of the two. Furthermore, whilst I have detailed two interviews where the entire dialogue occurred between the trainee in question and myself as supervisor, commonly other group members participate in this process as well. In conclusion, the overall aim of supervisors, on their own or with other group members, is to help anxious trainees: (1) acknowledge their anxiety; (2) identify and challenge the inferential distortions and irrational beliefs which underlie their anxiety; and (3) replace these with more accurate inferences and rational beliefs. When this is done successfully, trainees normally become less anxious, regularly present their audio tapes for supervision in a non-defensive manner and generally benefit greatly from supervisory feed-back.

References

BECK, A.T., RUSH, A.J., SHAW, B.F. and EMERY, G. (1979). *Cognitive Therapy of Depression.* New York: Guilford Press.

BURNS, D.D. (1980). *Feeling Good: The new mood therapy.* New York: William Morrow.

DRYDEN, W. (1981). Some uses of audio-tape procedures in counselling: a personal view. *Counselling*, April, No. 36, 14–17.

DRYDEN, W. (1984). Rational–emotive therapy (RET). In: W. Dryden (Ed.), *Individual Therapy in Britain.* London: Harper & Row.

DRYDEN, W., TROWER, P. and CASEY, A. (1983). A comprehensive approach to social skills training II: Contributions from rational–emotive therapy. *The Counsellor*, 3(7), 2–12.

ELLIS, A. (1972). Psychotherapy and the value of a human being. In: W. Davis (Ed.), *Value and Valuation: Aetiological studies in honor of Robert A. Hartman.* Knoxville: University of Tennessee Press.

ELLIS, A. (1977a). Irrational ideas. In: J.L. Wolfe and E. Brand (Eds), *Twenty Years of Rational Therapy.* New York: Institute for Rational Living.

ELLIS, A. (1977b). Fun as psychotherapy. *Rational Living*, 12, 2–9.

KADUSHIN, A. (1968). Games people play in supervision. *Social Work*, 13, 23–32.

LAZARUS, A. (1978). *In the Mind's Eye.* New York: Rawson.

YALOM, I.D. (1975). *The Theory and Practice of Group Psychotherapy*, 2nd edn. New Basic Books.

Chapter 7
The Rational–Emotive Counselling Sequence

In my work as a trainer of novice rational–emotive counsellors I had long considered that they lacked a clear step-by-step framework for the practice of basic REC. Prior to the development of this sequence, trainees observed live demonstrations of REC before being asked to practise this approach to counselling in peer counselling sessions (where trainees counsel each other on their genuine emotive problems). The problem was, however, that their observations were not informed by exposure to a clear sequence of the steps that needed to be followed for the practice of good REC. I thus developed, with help from Ray DiGiuseppe, a 13-step framework that outlines the sequence in which good REC needs to be practised. It was originally designed to enable trainees enrolled in REC training programmes to gain experience in practising REC in a peer counselling format. However, it can also be employed by REC trainees in their clinical work with clients. As such it is a good example of clear instructional training material developed to inform REC skills development. The framework was first published in 1990.

Two Caveats

It is important, at the outset, to note that this sequence applies when dealing with a *given* client problem. I will not consider how to deal with the situation where a client has several problems in this chapter but refer readers to Dryden (1990) for a discussion of this issue.

Also when reading this material, please note that the creative execution of the REC counselling sequence is done within the context of developing and maintaining a productive therapeutic alliance between you and your client, an issue which is again discussed in Dryden (1990).

The Sequence

Step 1: Ask for a problem

After you have greeted your client (in this case female), help her to discuss her reasons for coming for counselling and to talk about her problems in a fairly open-ended manner, and show empathic understanding of her position. Then ask her for a specific problem to work on. This might be the client's major problem or the problem that she wishes to start on first.

Step 2: Define and agree the target problem

It is important for you and your client to have a common understanding of what this particular problem is, and a shared understanding that this problem will be the focus for initial therapeutic exploration. The more specifically you can help your client to identify the nature of the problem, the more likely it is that you will then be successful in carrying out an assessment of this problem (in steps 3, 4 and 7). This is accomplished by using the ABC framework of REC, where A equals the activating event, or the client's inference about this event. B stands for the client's beliefs about the event, and C stands for the client's emotional and behavioural consequences of holding the belief at B.

Step 3: Assess C

This step in the REC sequence involves the assessment of C, the client's emotions and behaviour. It is important at this stage that you help her to focus on an inappropriate negative emotion, such as anger, depression, anxiety or feelings of hurt etc. You would also be advised to be on the look-out for self-defeating actions or behaviour, such as procrastination, addictions and so on. However, clients who report experiencing concern, or sadness in response to a loss, annoyance or some other kind of disappointment, and who are taking effective action and leading self-disciplined lives, are in fact handling themselves constructively. This follows from the observation that it is generally regarded as unrealistic for human beings to have neutral or positive feelings about negative events in their lives. Thus, it is important at this point to help your client to identify a self-defeating negative emotion, not a constructive negative emotion. At this step you can also assess your client's motivation to change her inappropriate negative emotion and encourage her to strive towards experiencing the more constructive negative appropriate emotion. This, however, can be done elsewhere in the assessment part of the sequence (i.e. between steps 3 and 6).

Step 4: Assess A

Once you have clarified what C is, you are now in a position to find out what your client specifically was disturbed about in the actual example you are assessing. It is important to realise that, when you assess A, you are not only trying to assess the objective aspects of that situation. This involves looking for your client's interpretations or inferences about A. Your major task here is to identify the most relevant interpretation or inference involved, the particular inference which triggered the client's emotional beliefs that in turn led to her disturbed feelings or behaviours at C.

Step 5: Determine the presence of secondary emotional problems and assess if necessary

It often transpires that clients have secondary emotional problems about their original emotional problems. For example, clients can often feel guilty about their anger, ashamed about their depression, anxious about their anxiety, guilty about their procrastination etc. Therefore, at this point in the process, or earlier if appropriate, it is important to determine whether or not your client does have a secondary emotional problem about her primary emotional problem. If she does have a secondary problem, then it is important to target this problem for treatment first before proceeding to deal with the primary problem if you consider that the secondary problem is going to interfere significantly with your work on the primary problem. So, if your client is feeling ashamed about her anger, for example, then those feelings of shame may interfere with and possibly block effective work on helping her overcome her anger, and thus shame (the secondary emotional problem) would be dealt with first in this case.

Step 6: Teach the B–C connection

Whether you are proceeding with your client's primary emotional problem, or whether you have switched and are now in the process of assessing a secondary emotional problem, the next stage in the rational–emotive counselling sequence is to help the client to understand the connection between her emotions and her beliefs. Specifically strive to help your client to understand that her emotions do not stem from the activating event which she is discussing, or her interpretations of this event, but from her beliefs and evaluations about these events or interpretations. If you fail to do this, your client will be puzzled by your emphasis on assessing her irrational beliefs. It is important, therefore, to bring out the connection between the Bs and Cs at the right stage in the rational–emotive counselling sequence.

Step 7: Assess irrational beliefs

Assuming that you have successfully assessed A and C, you are now in a position to help your client to identify the particular irrational beliefs that she has about the event or situation that brought about her problem at C. In particular, be on the lookout for the following.

'Demandingness'

Here your client will be making absolute demands about A in the form of 'musts', 'shoulds', 'oughts', 'have to's' etc.

'Awfulising'

Here, your client will be saying things like, 'It's awful that A occurred, and that's terrible, or horrible'.

Low frustration tolerance

Help your client to look for beliefs indicative of low frustration tolerance, or an attitude of 'I can't stand it'. Your client will frequently say that something was intolerable, or unbearable, or too hard to put up with etc.

Statements of damnation

Under this heading you will hear your client making global negative evaluations of herself, other people and/or the life conditions she is living under. These global statements of evaluation can be extreme, such as, 'I am a rotten person', or they may be less extreme but still basically irrational and insupportable because they involve a total, or global, evaluation of the self – which is, in reality, far too complex to be given such a rating or indeed, as you will see later, *any* kind of rating whatever. Thus, your client may, to use a less extreme example, insist that she is less worthy or less lovable as a result of what happened at A. This is still a global kind of rating, however, and if it occurs you will note it for later discussion.

Step 8: Connect irrational beliefs with C

Before proceeding to encourage your client to challenge her irrational beliefs, it is important, first of all, to help her to see the connection between her irrational beliefs and her disturbed emotions and behaviours at point C. If this is not done, or not done adequately, your client will not understand why you are now proceeding to encourage her to question her irrational beliefs. Even if you discussed the general connection between B and C at step 6, you still need to help your client to understand the specific connection between irrational beliefs and C at step 8.

Step 9: Dispute irrational beliefs

The major goals of disputing at this point in the REC treatment process is to encourage your client to understand that her irrational beliefs are unproductive, i.e. that they lead to self-defeating emotions which are illogical and inconsistent with reality. Moreover, these irrational beliefs cannot be supported by any factual evidence or scientific reasoning. By contrast, rational alternatives to these beliefs are productive, logical, consistent with reality and self-helping. They will not get the client into trouble, but instead, help her to achieve her goals in life with the minimum of emotional and behavioural upsets. More specifically, the goals of disputing are to help your client to understand the following.

Musts

There is no evidence in support of her absolute demands, while evidence does exist for her preferences.

'Awfulising'

What your client has defined as awful, i.e. 100 per cent bad, cannot be upheld and that in reality it will lie within a scale of badness from 0 to 99.9. Only one thing could be regarded as totally bad, and that is death itself; but even that is debatable since it is possible to regard death as preferable to dying slowly in excruciating agony with no hope whatsoever of relief. Often when you are helping your client to understand that, if she rates something as 100 per cent bad, she is really saying that nothing else in the world could possibly be worse. Once your client can see that this is absurd, she can more readily accept that her evaluation is greatly exaggerated.

Low frustration tolerance

Your client can always stand what she thinks she cannot stand, and can be reasonably happy, although not as happy as she would be if the difficult situation she has outlined at point A changed for the better.

Damnation or making global negative ratings of self, others or the world

This cannot legitimately be done because humans are human, i.e. fallible beings, and are not in any way damnable no matter what they do or do not do. Further, human beings are too complex to be given a single global rating that completely summarises their total being. Statements like 'I am worthless', for example, mean that I am totally without worth or value to myself or to anybody else and possess no redeeming features whatever. How could this ever be substantiated? Obviously, it could not. Similarly, the world, too, is not damnable and contains a mixture of good, bad and other complex aspects which cannot possibly be given some kind of global rating. Once you can get your client to understand and accept this, she will become less inclined to deify or devilify herself or others, and more able to accept herself and others as fallible, but non-damnable, human beings.

At the end of step 9, if you have been successful in helping your client to dispute her irrational beliefs, you will perceive a new awareness in your client of the lack of any real evidence to support her previously held irrational beliefs and an acceptance of these beliefs and evaluations as illogical and both self- and relationship-defeating. At the same time, you will observe the gradual emergence of the client's appreciation of why the new rational beliefs are logical, reality based and self-helping, as well as potentially relationship enhancing with others. A word of caution, however. Your client's newly acquired rational beliefs are unlikely to become deep, solid convictions overnight. She may say things like, 'I understand what you are saying, and I think I believe it, but I don't yet feel it in my gut'. It takes time for your client's new beliefs about herself and the world to sink in, so to speak, and to become an integral part of her psychological make-up. For that reason, the remaining steps in the REC process are devised to help your client internalise her rational beliefs to the point that she can say with conviction, 'Yes, I now understand what you are saying in my gut as well as in my head and I can now act on this rational understanding'.

Step 10: Prepare your client to deepen her conviction in her rational beliefs

At this point, before you encourage your client to put into practice her new learning, it is important to help her to understand that long-term therapeutic change does involve a good deal of hard work on her part if she is ever going to deepen her new rational convictions to the point that they become virtually a new rational philosophy of living.

Step 11: Encourage your client to put her learning into practice

You are now in a position to help your client to put into practice a variety of cognitive, emotive, imagery and behavioural homework assignments. These are discussed with your client and she plays an active role in choosing assignments that are most relevant for her. For further information on such assignments see Ellis and Dryden (1987).

Step 12: Check the homework assignment

The next step in the REC sequence is for you to check your client's reactions to doing the homework assignment you set. This may have been a shame-attacking exercise, or some other activity which your client has been reluctant to face because of some emotional block arising from irrational beliefs concerning the situation. It is important to ascertain if she faced the situation that she agreed to face and whether or not she changed her irrational beliefs in the process of doing so. If the assignment was not carried out satisfactorily, reassign the task after verifying whether your client's failure was due to the continuing existence in her mind of those irrational beliefs and evaluations which the exercise was designed to undermine in the first place. Should that turn out to be the case, once more invite your client to identify and challenge the irrational beliefs that sidetracked her from carrying out the assigned task. When this has been done, reassign the task and monitor the result.

Step 13: Facilitate the working through process

Once your client has achieved a measure of success in changing some of her core irrational beliefs by successfully executing the relevant homework assignments, go on from there to help your client to develop other assignments designed to help her gain experience in behaving in accordance with her emerging new rational philosophy. Thus, if your client has successfully challenged the irrational beliefs concerning public disapproval in social situations, help her to maximise her gains by designing homework assignments aimed at helping her to recognise and dispute any irrational beliefs she might have about disapproval in other situations, such as work relations with colleagues or personal relations with significant others. Your aim is to help your client not only to recognise and rip up her irrational beliefs about whatever situation or problem is currently troubling her, but to show her how to generalise her new learning to any future problem that she might experience. Once your client has gained experience and achieved success at challenging and disputing the irrational beliefs underlying one particular problem, she is more likely to be able to take on greater responsibility for initiating the REC sequence with other problems. At the end of rational–emotive counselling, the degree of success achieved by both you and your client may be gauged by the extent to which she demonstrates the ability to live a more satisfying life with few, if any, of the emotional hang-ups with which she began counselling originally.

However, even the brightest and most enthusiastic of clients may, on occasions, slip back into their old self-defeating ways. The answer? Back to basics you go! It is on occasions like this that you will see the emergence of what I referred to previously as secondary problems. Here, your client upsets herself because she has experienced some kind of a relapse. For example, your client may have felt guilty over some act of commission or omission and is now denigrating herself for feeling guilty. 'How stupid of me to upset myself again, and after all I've learned about REC! Boy, what a dumbo that makes me!'

If your client reports a relapse, consider it as normal, as par for the course. In any case, nobody is completely rational. We can think, feel and behave rationally most of the time and rarely upset ourselves over the various hassles and problems of living in a complex world. But can we realistically expect to be like that all of the time? Hardly! Assure your client, therefore, that to take two steps forward and then one back, is the common experience. Do not waste time overly commiserating with your client. Instead, repeat the 13-step REC sequence. Help your client to understand that staying emotionally healthy does not come about automatically, but requires continuous work and practice before the REC philosophy she has been trying hard to assimilate actually becomes an integral part of her life.

Show your client that there is no reason why she absolutely must not feel ashamed or dejected because some old emotional problem has returned to plague her. Encourage her to accept that this is normal, a natural part of our human fallibility. Emphasise (once more) that we all have innate tendencies to think in absolutistic, *must*urbatory ways and that we are all naturally crooked thinkers; it comes easy to us! At this point retrace your steps and use the ABC framework to re-orient your client back to the task of disputing her irrational beliefs. Your client already knows that her previous problem(s) become established through her habitually thinking the irrational thoughts that created it. So, go after those irrational beliefs with your client. Get your client to identify, challenge and dispute them until she is thoroughly convinced of their falseness. Encourage her to look for variations of the main irrational beliefs and to understand *why* they are irrational and cannot be accepted as true, regardless of what form they are presented in. Help your client to keep looking, and looking, for her absolutistic demands upon herself and others, the *shoulds*, *oughts* and *musts*, and to replace them with flexible, non-dogmatic desires and preferences.

Finally, stress the importance, once more, of your client acting against her irrational beliefs until she becomes comfortable doing what she was unrealistically afraid to try. Show your client how she can put muscle into her newly acquired REC philosophy by means of self-management techniques, rational—emotive imagery exercises and shame-attacking exercises (see Ellis and Dryden, 1987) until she convinces herself that she really can make headway against even her most stubborn self-defeating beliefs and habits. When your client reaches the stage where she can easily recognise and distinguish her appropriate from her inappropriate feelings, understand why the difference is important, and demonstrate that she can uproot the shoulds, oughts and musts that underlie her inappropriate feelings, you may assume that your client is well on her way to regaining effective emotional control of her life.

References

DRYDEN, W. (1990). *Rational—Emotive Counselling in Action*. London: Sage.
ELLIS, A. and DRYDEN, W. (1987). *The Practice of Rational—Emotive Therapy*. New York: Springer.

Chapter 8
Audio-tape Supervision by Mail: A Rational–Emotive Perspective

In this chapter (published in 1984) I outline how I use therapeutic alliance theory as a framework to guide my comments when I am supervising REC trainees' counselling tapes through the mail. Much of my REC supervision is done by mail because trainees either live in another part of the country or abroad. Such supervision needs to be well structured and to provide feed-back both on trainees' REC skills and on more general therapeutic issues. I have found therapeutic alliance theory to be helpful in both respects.

Introduction

The aims of this chapter are: (1) to describe my approach to supervising by mail the audio-taped counselling sessions of trainee rational–emotive counsellors and (2) to discuss some of the issues that arise from this mode of supervision.

The rational–emotive theory of emotions posits that emotional experience is based on evaluative thinking. Two major types of such thinking are identified: rational and irrational. Rational evaluations refer to appraisals of liking or disliking which are stated as personal preferences. Irrational evaluations occur when these personal preferences are escalated to unqualified, absolute demands. Such demands can be made on ourselves, other people and the world. When people rationally desire or prefer something, they further conclude that if they don't get it: (1) it is really inconvenient but not the end of the world and (2) they are fallible humans with failings and inadequacies, but not worthless, damnable individuals. Consequent to holding this rational belief, they will feel frustrated, concerned, sad or sorry – emotions which are self-enhancing because they are likely to motivate the individuals to try and change the situation or help them to adjust if change is not possible. However, when people escalate their preferences to demands, namely that since they want something, they absolutely must get it, they will further conclude: (1) it is awful if they do not get it and (2) they are worthless or bad people for failing. Consequent to holding this irrational belief, they are likely to experience anxiety, depression, shame and guilt – emotions which are self-defeating in that they generally impede people from changing the situation or adapting, if change is not possible. Rational–emotive theory further posits that individuals can take an almost limitless range of desires, e.g. for love, approval, comfort, control, competence and clarity, and escalate these to absolute demands. Furthermore, dysfunctional behavioural patterns are deemed to stem from those irrational beliefs.

As I have mentioned elsewhere, the major tasks of the rational–emotive counsellor are:

> (1) to help the patient to share his theoretical stance that the patient's disturbance has attitudinal antecedents, (2) to help the patient see that changes in belief will promote emotional and behavioural well-being and (3) to help the patient acknowledge that he had better continually work at changing his irrational beliefs by cognitive, imaginal and behavioural disputations.   (Dryden, 1982, p.17)

The major tasks of rational–emotive supervisors, whether they are supervising trainee counsellors in person or by mail are: (1) to give them feed-back on their understanding of the fundamentals of rational–emotive theory as this is manifested in clinical interventions and (2) to give them feed-back on more general clinical skills (Wessler and Ellis, 1980). This dual purpose is implicit in the work of rational–emotive supervisors no matter what training programme trainee counsellors are undertaking.

Most of my supervision work of trainee rational–emotive counsellors occurs with those who are undergoing the associate fellowship training scheme which is sponsored by the Institute of Rational–Emotive Therapy in New York. In order to qualify for this programme, trainee counsellors must: (1) have participated in a 5-day primary certificate programme in the fundamentals of rational–emotive counselling and (2) hold a recognised counselling, psychology or psychotherapy qualification in the country in which they are employed. To gain associate fellow status, candidates have to (1) participate in two 5-day workshops where various topics in advanced rational–emotive theory and practice are covered and (2) submit 25 of their counselling tapes for supervision. Furthermore their supervisors must testify as to their competence. Candidates are strongly encouraged to submit their tapes to no less than three supervisors, although this regulation may be waived in countries which do not have many accredited supervisors, such as Britain. My experience in supervising trainee counsellors has been almost exclusively limited to supervision of tapes by mail. I have supervised counsellors from London, Dublin, Bristol, Sheffield, Nova Scotia in Canada and various cities in America. The working alliance between myself and trainee counsellors in these programmes is founded on the assumption that I will be giving them feed-back on their tapes from a rational–emotive perspective. I encourage supervisees to send me, according to their opinion, both good and bad examples of their work. Occasionally, supervisees only select tapes from counselling sessions that are going well. In this event, I usually confront such supervisees asking them to reflect on the possible underlying motivations for such behaviour, e.g. need for approval, need to be seen as competent etc.

Whether I am supervising trainees in person or by mail, I believe that listening to audio tapes of counselling sessions is paramount to the process of supervision, especially in rational–emotive counselling. Listening to tapes allows me to hear what trainee counsellors say, how they say it, when they say it and if they say it (Garcia, 1976). In my experience, trainee counsellors' accounts of counselling sessions are also important for supervisors to elicit, but on their own do not provide adequate information concerning what actually transpired in the sessions. Obviously video tapes of counselling sessions would provide the non-verbal channel missing from audio tapes. However, such technology is expensive and tape compatibility problems which exist mean that video-tape supervision by mail is not feasible.

The obvious disadvantage of supervising audio-taped counselling sessions by mail is that the immediate dialogue which face-to-face supervision provides is missing. I find that whilst I endeavour to ask supervisees questions while taping my supervisory comments, I experience a tendency to give my own opinions about the counselling session more frequently than I would in face-to-face supervision. On this point, I agree with Garcia (1976) who has said: 'It seems to me that you are a good supervisor not by the answers you give but by the questions you ask.'

Another major disadvantage of supervision by mail is that there is an inevitable delay between trainees conducting counselling sessions and receiving supervision on them. I endeavour to supervise tapes on the day I receive them or no later than the day after receipt. However, it is still doubtful that supervisees will receive my supervision before seeing their clients again.

However, there are advantages to supervising audio tapes by mail. First, it enables trainees to receive comments on their work where distance precludes face-to-face supervision. It is unrealistic to expect one of my supervisees from Dublin, for example, to fly over for a 1-hour supervision session, there being no rational–emotive supervisors in Dublin. Secondly, it enables trainees to get feed-back from a supervisor with a good reputation where distance is again a problem. Thus, if I was limited to face-to-face supervision I would not have been supervised by Albert Ellis as part of my own training programme. Thirdly, this form of supervision allows supervisors to conduct supervision at times convenient to them. Thus, I prefer to supervise tapes late at night at a time when I feel most creative.

There are three major ways of supervising audio tapes by mail. Supervisors can: (1) listen to an entire session and then either write or tape their comments; (2) give ongoing written or taped comments while listening to the session; and (3) listen to the entire session first, give general comments and then listen to the session again giving ongoing supervision. My own preference is to tape my comments and provide whatever type of supervision my supervisees find most helpful and can financially afford.

Since I am supervising tapes by mail, I find it even more important to involve my trainees in the supervisory process as much as I can. More specifically I encourage them to formulate their own goals for supervision. I thus ask them at the beginning of our supervisory relationship what they would like to achieve from my supervision and, more specifically, I encourage them to address themselves to concrete concerns about a particular counselling session. I ask them to specify what strengths they demonstrated in the counselling session and how, in retrospect, they would have conducted the session differently. I prefer my supervisees to send me several tapes from a particular ongoing counselling case rather than to send me isolated tapes from several cases. This helps me to hear how my trainees conduct counselling over time and allows me to address this issue in my supervisory feedback. My overall strategy, then, is to stimulate my supervisees' thinking so that they can learn in time to supervise themselves. However, I do believe that it is important for even experienced counsellors to remain in supervision throughout their career. Thus, I have a co-supervisory relationship with a colleague in Chicago with whom I regularly exchange tapes for supervision.

Therapeutic Alliance: A Framework for Supervision

The framework I use for supervising trainee rational–emotive counsellors is one based on recent theorising on the three dimensions of the therapeutic alliance (Dryden, 1982). From this viewpoint, effective counselling of whatever orientation occurs when: (1) the counsellor and client have a good working interpersonal relationship (the *bond* dimension); (2) both counsellor and client are working together towards helping the client realise his or her goals (the *goal* dimension); and (3) both counsellor and client acknowledge their respective tasks and believe that such tasks are sufficient for the client to reach such goals (the *task* dimension).

Feed-back on therapeutic 'bonds'

In giving my supervisees feed-back on the quality of the therapeutic bond between them and their clients, I initially address myself to the core therapeutic conditions described by Rogers (1957). First, I pay attention

to *counsellor empathy*. I listen in particular to: (1) whether my
supervisees encourage their clients to state fully their problems as they
see them; (2) whether and how accurately they communicate such
understanding, i.e. do they work from their clients' data or do they allow
rational–emotive theory to distort such data inappropriately. Secondly, I
listen closely to the extent to which they *accept* their clients as fallible
human beings – are there any signs that they adopt a judgemental attitude
towards their clients? Thirdly, I listen for signs that they are not being
genuine in their encounters with their clients – are they inappropriately
adopting a façade?

It is important to realise that Rogers' (1957) original hypothesis stated
that the important mechanism for change was the extent to which such
counsellor-offered conditions are perceived by clients rather than by
external observers (in this case, supervisors). Nevertheless, if supervisors
put themselves in a particular client's frame of reference, such feed-back
may have increased reliability. I not only give my supervisees feed-back
on these attitudes but also ask them to reflect on what intrapsychic
obstacles might exist in them that could block the therapeutic expression
of such attitude. Here, as elsewhere on similar matters, the supervisees are
left to do such reflection on their own (or perhaps with their own
counsellors!).

I then address myself to the extent to which supervisees have developed
a collaborative working relationship with their clients. Here I use the
concept of 'collaborative empiricism' developed by Beck et al.'s (1979)
work in cognitive therapy. The therapeutic style of collaborative empiricism is one in which counsellors endeavour to explain to clients the
rationale for most of their interventions. Counsellors and clients set an
agenda at most sessions. Counsellors help their clients identify and
question maladaptive cognitions through guided discovery. They frequently pause and ask for feed-back from clients to determine the impact
of their therapeutic interventions, and basically clue clients into most of
what is happening in the therapeutic endeavour. I particularly listen for
instances where my supervisees do not involve their clients in this way
and ask them to reflect on whether this indicates a lack of skill in this area
or the presence of dysfunctional attitudes such as low frustration tolerance.

I next concern myself with the question of whether my supervisees'
interactive styles present clients with opportunities to reflect on their own
dysfunctional interpersonal styles or whether, in fact, the interactive styles
of supervisees actually reinforce their clients' interpersonal problems. For
example, whilst rational–emotive counselling is an active–directive form
of psychotherapy, it is possible for the counsellor to become too active,
which is contraindicated particularly with a passive client because it tends
to reinforce the client's passivity and hence his or her personal and
interpersonal problems.

Finally, I listen for signs of anxiety in my supervisees' interaction with clients and try to help them identify its attitudinal determinants. In my experience, common counsellor problems in this area revolve around the following issues: counsellor need for client approval, counsellor need for competence and to be right, and counsellor need to control the interaction. The effects of such irrational beliefs are invariably harmful for clients and early termination, client deterioration and interminable counselling are the common manifestations of these counsellor problems. In such cases, I usually recommend that the supervisee in question seeks psychotherapeutic help to resolve such obstacles to the conduct of effective counselling.

Feed-back on 'goals'

Effective counselling is deemed to occur when counsellor and client work towards realising the client's goals. Thus, first, I listen to hear whether my supervisees have elicited their clients' goals for change. Since this often involves considerable negotiation between counsellor and client, I listen for signs that supervisees initiate such negotiation and focus on how they handle the process which usually occurs at the initial stage of counselling. I also listen to hear whether supervisees help their clients to set goals for a particular session and whether attainment of such goals are feasible. In my experience, effective rational–emotive counsellors help their clients see that they can reach their ultimate goals by means of reaching a series of mediating goals. I thus listen for client goals at three levels: (1) session goals, (2) mediating goals and (3) ultimate goals, and most importantly I listen for evidence that counsellors help their clients see the links between them.

The major danger of setting goals at the initial stage of rational–emotive counselling is that trainee counsellors then assume that these goals are relevant to clients for the entire course of counselling. Since their relevance often becomes outdated, I listen for evidence that supervisees periodically review client goals, and whether they strive to understand the psychological processes underlying the shifts that occur.

I listen to what level of goal specificity supervisees are prepared to work with. Clients can state their goals very broadly, e.g. 'I want to be happy', or very specifically, e.g. 'I want to meet three girls by August 24th'. Counsellor errors occur at both levels of specificity. I encourage trainee counsellors to consider the value of medium range goals, e.g. 'I want to be able to approach girls, still feel concerned about being rejected but without feeling devastated by the prospect'.

Finally, I listen for evidence that supervisees have accepted goals that realistically cannot be achieved by counselling. In my experience as a supervisor these form two clusters. The first cluster of unrealistic goals accepted by trainee counsellors are those that would be more appropriate for computers not humans. Thus, clients, whose goals are never to feel anxiety, depression, anger, or who always want to be happy, are doomed to disappointment by even the most talented counsellor. The second cluster of unrealistic client goals accepted by supervisees involves changes in other people or circumstances. This area is more complicated because counsellors had better help clients try non-manipulatively to influence others and circumstances where appropriate, without appearing to promise that such changes are possible. Thus, I encourage my supervisees to help clients deal with unchanging others or circumstances first before discussing attempts to bring about change in them. This point is particularly pertinent to the field of couple counselling.

Feed-back on 'tasks'

The tasks of rational–emotive counsellors can be grouped into a number of major clusters. The first important cluster of tasks is concerned with *structuring* therapy. When listening to tapes, I focus and comment on how supervisees structure therapy for their clients. Most specifically, I listen to whether and how supervisees execute the following tasks: (1) the task of outlining their own tasks and that of their clients in counselling; (2) the task of specifying the existing boundaries which frame therapeutic work (e.g. time, geography, frequency of contact and finance); and (3) the task of eliciting and dealing with clients' expectations and misconceptions about counselling. I further concern myself with how supervisees structure each particular counselling session. Questions which are at the forefront of my mind here are the following:

1. Do counsellors set an agenda and/or help clients prioritise items and how do they do this?
2. Do they use the agenda in a flexible way, dealing with important items that emerge during the course of the session or do they stick rigidly to the agenda, no matter what?
3. Do they deal with their clients' experiences concerning any homework assignments arising from the prior session and in particular elicit and deal with reasons for non-completion of such assignments?
4. Do they elicit their clients' cooperation throughout the session and elicit feed-back from clients during and at the end of the session?
5. Do they explain their rationale for the interventions that they have made in the session or do they intervene without explanation?

The second cluster of tasks concerns *assessment*. Effective rational– emotive counselling (REC) depends heavily on adequate assessment of client problems. Thus, I pay a lot of attention to this phase of therapy. Assessment is best carried out in REC when trainee counsellors ask clients for specific examples of their problems. Having elicited specific examples of their clients' problems, including the most relevant inferences about the pertinent activating events, supervisees preferably should turn their attention to the elicitation of clear statements of clients' emotional experiences. Vague formulations of emotional experiences, such as 'I felt upset' or 'I felt bad' are to be avoided, since they do not provide enough clarity for identification of mediating irrational beliefs. If clients' problems are behavioural in nature, clear assessment of behavioural patterns is indicated. Supervisees preferably should then proceed to help their clients see that irrational beliefs underlie their dysfunctional emotional experiences and/or behavioural patterns. I then listen for evidence that trainee counsellors elicit their clients' reactions to this formulation of their problems. I give clear feed-back to supervisees concerning their errors at this stage, since mistakes here are bound to lead to road-blocks later on in the session. Because a limited number of irrational beliefs are likely to underlie many client problems, I listen for evidence that trainee counsellors help their clients see links between their problems, thus enabling clients to begin to assess their own problems in rational–emotive terms.

Another important component in this cluster concerns assessment of client progress on all pertinent problems. Ongoing assessment of progress can be included as an ever-present item on the therapeutic agenda or periodic review sessions can be conducted. Trainee rational–emotive counsellors often do not carry out this ongoing assessment and thus lose track of their clients' current status. I thus often recommend that my supervisees do this routinely. Ongoing assessment has the additional advantage of providing opportunities for reformulation of client goals. One particular feature of assessment which trainee counsellors often overlook is thorough assessment of suicidal ideation and intent in depressed patients. If it is dealt with at all, supervisees are often wary of dealing with this issue directly, preferring to ask such questions as: 'Have you thought of doing something silly?' Listening to how trainee counsellors deal with suicide issues often reveals their own distorted inferences and irrational beliefs concerning these issues. I thus frequently ask my supervisees to reflect on their own possible dysfunctional attitudes concerning the introduction of the topic of assessing suicidal ideation and intent. They report such attitudes as: 'I didn't want to upset the client', 'I was too embarrassed to talk about it' and 'I didn't want to put ideas into her head'. When such attitudes are expressed, an ongoing period of dialogue is highly desirable and, if feasible, I encourage the supervisee in question to telephone me so this can occur. If this is not feasible then I recommend that my supervisee contacts a clinician who is experienced in treating suicidal clients for consultation.

The third cluster of tasks concerns helping clients to re-examine distorted inferences and irrational beliefs. Ideally, trainee counsellors involve clients in this process as much as possible by means of Socratic dialogues. The purpose here is to stimulate clients' own thinking concerning the dysfunctional nature of their cognitive processes. Common trainee errors here usually involve counsellors explaining to their clients why an inference is distorted or why a belief is irrational, and providing them with plausible alternatives instead of allowing those clients who are capable of performing this task to re-examine for themselves the untenable bases for these dysfunctional cognitions. Particularly while trainee counsellors engage their clients in the process of re-examining their irrational beliefs, I listen for evidence that they help their clients see the link between the alternative rational belief and their realistic goals, i.e. how they would like to feel and behave. It is only when clients see this link that they are motivated to work and change their irrational beliefs. Again trainee counsellors often omit this stage.

During the re-examination stage of counselling, trainee rational–emotive counsellors can use a variety of cognitive, imagery, emotive and behavioural techniques (Wessler and Wessler, 1980). When I listen to the techniques employed by supervisees, I focus and comment on the following:

1. I comment on the *variety of techniques* that my supervisees employ over time. Here the greater the variety of techniques which they have in their armamentarium, the more likely it is that they are going to be successful in helping a broad range of clients. If trainee counsellors only use a limited range of techniques I try to ascertain the reasons for this. If they indicate that they only know a certain range of techniques, I often suggest others and model their possible applications. However, trainees are often aware of other techniques but do not use them for other reasons. For example, one supervisee claimed that she did not use imagery techniques because she had great difficulty imagining events herself. My task here is to help supervisees identify and correct such blocks.

2. I comment on my supervisees' *skill* at using particular techniques. Here I both directly comment on the way trainee counsellors employ the techniques and ask them to think of different ways of using them. I may model other ways of using such techniques or suggest to my supervisees that they listen to counselling sessions in the Institute for Rational–Emotive Therapy's tape library in which such techniques are skilfully demonstrated.

3. I comment on the *relevant* use of particular techniques. Sometimes trainee counsellors employ techniques skilfully but inappropriately. Here supervisees often do not give enough thought to the use of techniques with specific clients with whom they are working. This danger is partially avoided if they explain adequately their rationale for

using particular techniques and gain client cooperation beforehand. If clients cannot see a technique's relevance, this is one sign that perhaps it should not be used. In addition, trainee counsellors' choice of technique may be inappropriate for the modality of experience concerned. For example, if a particular client's irrational belief is manifested in imagery, then re-examination through verbal dialogue may not be as relevant as a carefully selected imagery method. Knowledge of clients' dominant modalities is important here.

The final cluster of tasks concerns the use of *homework assignments*. Homework exercises are important in rational–emotive counselling because their appropriate use helps clients to generalise their learning from the counselling situation to everyday experience. I listen carefully to the following:

1. I focus on the amount of time that trainee counsellors devote to discussing possible assignments with their clients. A common fault here is that trainees devote too little time to this and consequently terminate the session by either unilaterally assigning homework exercises – a procedure which often increases the possibility of client resistance – or by dropping the subject altogether. Here I usually ask my supervisees to consider how much time to devote to the process of assigning homework and to monitor closely their performance on this parameter.
2. I focus on how adequately trainee counsellors prepare their clients for doing assignments. Important considerations here concern:
   (a) the relevance of the tasks to the issues that have hopefully been thoroughly assessed and re-examined in the session in question;
   (b) clients seeing clearly the potential value of such assignments to their mediating and ultimate goals;
   (c) clients being fully involved by trainee counsellors in the negotiation of homework assignments.
3. I listen carefully for evidence that supervisees have tried to uncover possible obstacles to the successful completion of assignments by asking their clients in advance to speculate on what might stop them from carrying them out. If relevant information is uncovered by such inquiry, I listen to how trainees help their clients overcome such obstacles in the session. If this information is not asked for, I suggest to them that they think of the value of doing this routinely.
4. I listen for evidence that trainee counsellors engage clients in rehearsal of homework assignments either in imagery or using behavioural rehearsal in the session. This enables clients to gain some related experience of doing assignments and may in itself unearth further dysfunctional cognitions which might prevent clients from completing such tasks in their everyday situation.
5. I listen to the specificity of negotiated homework assignments. The

more tasks have been specified, the more likely it is that clients will be able successfully to carry them out.

6. I listen to the breadth of assignments suggested by trainees counsellors to their clients over the supervisory period. Preferably, if appropriate, a wide range of behavioural, emotive, written and imagery assignments should be used during counselling. If trainees are employing a narrow range of tasks, I try and discern the reasons for this and encourage them to think about remedying this.

In addition, throughout the supervisory period, I encourage my supervisees to encourage their clients to move towards independence so that they in fact acquire the skills to be their own counsellors. If this is not done, I try and discover the reasons and encourage trainees to reflect on possible motivations that they might have for encouraging dependence. I attempt to sensitise my supervisees to the problem of client resistance to change and to possible reasons for this. Resistance may stem from client problems, counsellor problems, poor counsellor skills or their interaction.

Finally, I endeavour to communicate my points to supervisees in the form of hypotheses for them to consider and possibly test. I encourage them to give me feed-back on any suggestions that I have made and on my style of supervision in general so that I can fit the supervisory experience to individual supervisee requirements.

References

BECK, A.T., RUSH, A.J., SHAW, B.F. and EMERY, G. (1979). *Cognitive Therapy of Depression*. New York: Guilford Press.

DRYDEN, W. (1982). The therapeutic alliance: conceptual issues and some research findings. *The Midland Journal of Psychotherapy*, 1, 14–19.

GARCIA, E. (1976). Supervision of therapists. Unpublished lecture given at the Institute for Advanced Study of Rational–Emotive Therapy, New York City, July 11th.

ROGERS, C.R. (1957). The necessary and sufficient conditions of therapeutic personality change. *Journal of Consulting Psychology*, 21, 95–103.

WESSLER, R.A. and WESSLER, R.L. (1980). *The Principles and Practice of Rational–Emotive Therapy*. San Francisco: Jossey-Bass.

WESSLER, R.L. and ELLIS, A. (1980). Supervision in rational–emotive therapy. In: A.K. Hess (Ed.), *Psychotherapy Supervision*. New York: Wiley.

Index